Lizzie Doten

Poems From the Inner Life

Fourth Edition

Lizzie Doten

Poems From the Inner Life
Fourth Edition

ISBN/EAN: 9783744704878

Printed in Europe, USA, Canada, Australia, Japan

Cover: Foto ©Thomas Meinert / pixelio.de

More available books at **www.hansebooks.com**

POEMS

FROM

THE INNER LIFE.

BY

LIZZIE DOTEN.

"And my soul from out that shadow
Hath been lifted evermore." Poe.

"The kingdom of Heaven is within you."

FOURTH EDITION.

BOSTON:
WILLIAM WHITE AND COMPANY,
"BANNER OF LIGHT" OFFICE,
158 WASHINGTON STREET.
1865.

CONTENTS.

(iii)

A WORD TO THE WORLD.

In presenting this volume to the public, I trust that I may be allowed, without incurring the charge of egotism, to say somewhat concerning my spiritual experience, and the manner in which these poems were originated. I am, in a measure, under the necessity of doing this, lest some over-anxious friend, or would-be critic, should undertake the work for me, and thereby place me, either unconsciously or intentionally, in a false position before the public.

By the advice of those invisible intelligences, whose presence and power I freely acknowledge, seconded by my own judgment, I have given to this work the title of "Poems from

the Inner Life;" for, aside from the external
phenomena of Modern Spiritualism, — which,
compared to the great principles underlying
them, are but mere froth and foam on the
ocean of Truth, — I have realized that in the
mysterious depths of the Inner Life, all souls
can hold communion with those invisible beings, who are our companions both in Time and
Eternity. My vision has been dim and indistinct, my hearing confused by the jarring discords of earthly existence, and my utterances
of a wisdom, higher than my own, impeded by
my selfish conceits and vain imaginings. Yet,
notwithstanding all this, the solemn convictions
of my spiritual surroundings, and the mutual
ties of interest still existing between souls,
"whether in the body or out of the body,"
have been indelibly impressed upon me. From
such experiences I have learned — in a sense
hitherto unknown — that "the kingdom of
Heaven is within me." I know that many sincere and earnest souls will decide at once, in

the integrity of their well-trained intellects, that this claim to an intercourse with the invisible world is an extravagant assumption, and has no foundation in truth. To such I would say, I shall make no effort to persuade your reason and judgment. I only offer to you as a suggestion, that which has been realized by me in my spiritual experience, and has become to me an abiding truth, full of strength for the present, and hope for the future. When your souls sincerely hunger after such a revelation, you will seek for it, and according to your need, you will be filled therewith. Until then, you and I, regarding things from a different point of view, must inevitably understand them differently. There are various cups which Humanity must drink of, and "baptisms which it must be baptized with," and this manifestation of Truth, of which I am but one of the humble representatives, has laid its controlling hand upon me; for what purpose, in the mysterious results which lie concealed in the future, I cannot tell — I only know that it is so.

Looking back upon my experience, I cannot doubt that I — with many others — was destined to this phase of development, and designed for this peculiar work, before I knew conscious being. My brain was fashioned, and my nervous system finely strung, so that I should inevitably catch the thrill of the innumerable voices resounding through the universe, and translate their messages into human language, as coherently and clearly as my imperfections would allow. The early influences of my childhood, the experiences of later years, and more than all, that unutterable yearning for Beauty and Harmony, which I felt dimly conscious was somewhere in the universe, all tended to drive me back from the world, which would not and could not give me what I asked, to the revelations of my inner life, — to the "Heaven within me." It was only through the cultivation of my spiritual nature that "spiritual things were to be discerned," and the stern necessity of my life was the Teacher which finally educated me into the perception of Truth.

I turn back to the memories of my childhood — to that long course of trying experiences through which I passed, guided by strange and invisible influences; and that whole course of discipline has for me now a peculiar significance. Those who were near and dear to me, and who were most familiar with my habits of life, knew little of my intense spiritual experience. I was too much afraid of being ridiculed and misunderstood to dare give any expression to the strange and indefinable emotions within me. Such ones, however, may call to mind the child who often, through the long winter evenings, sat in profound silence by the fireside, with her head and face enveloped in her apron, to exclude, as far as possible, all external sight and sound. What I heard and saw then but dimly returns to me; but even then the revelations from the "Heaven within" had commenced, and succeeding years have so strengthened and confirmed my vision, that such scenes have become to me living truths and blessed realities. The

"Heaven" that "lay about me in my infancy" sent its rich glow through my childhood, and sheds its mystic brightness upon the pathway of my riper years.

Often, in the retirement of a small closet, I spent hours in total darkness, lying prostrate on the floor, beating the waves of the mysterious Infinite that rolled in a stormy flood over me, and with prayers and tears beseeching deliverance from my blindness and seeming unbelief. Then, when by my earnestness the spirit had become stronger than the flesh, I would gradually fall into a deep trance, from which I would arise strengthened and consoled by the assurance — from whence I could not tell — that somewhere in the future I should find all the life, and light, and freedom that my soul desired. The only evidence or knowledge which those around me received of such visitations was occasionally a poem — some of them written so early in life, that the childish chirography rendered them almost illegible. Because of these early productions, it has been asserted that my claim to any individual spirit-influence was either a falsehood or delusion. I will only say in reply, that there is no need of entering upon any argument on the subject. I claim both a general and particular inspiration. They do not, by any means, conflict; and what I do not receive from one, comes from the other. For the very reason that I have natural poetic tendencies, I attract influences of a kindred nature; and when I desire it, or they will to do so, they cast their characteristic inspirations upon me, and I give them utterance according to my ability. It is often as difficult to decide what is the action of one's own intellect and what is spirit-influence, as it is in our ordinary associations to determine what is original with ourselves and what we have received from circumstances or contact with the mind of others. Yet, nevertheless, there are cases where the distinction is so evident that it is not to be doubted. Only one or two such well-attest-

ed instances is sufficient to establish the theory.
I am not willing to ignore one faculty or power
of my being for the sake of proving a favorite idea; and, on the contrary, I cannot conscientiously deny that, in the mysteries of my
inner life, I have been acted upon decidedly
and directly by disembodied intelligences, and
this, sometimes, by an inspiration characteristic
of the individual, or by a psychological influence
similar to that whereby mind acts upon mind
in the body. Under such influences I have
not necessarily lost my individuality, or become wholly unconscious. I was, for the time
being, like a harp in the hands of superior
powers, and just in proportion as my entire
nature was attuned to thrill responsive to their
touch, did I give voice and expression to their
unwritten music. They furnished the inspiration, but it was of necessity modified by the
nature and character of the instrument upon
which they played, for the most skilful musi-
cian cannot change the tone of a harp to the

sound of a trumpet, though he may give a characteristic expression of himself through either.

The presence and influence of these powers is to me no new or recent occurrence, although I may not have understood them in the same light as I do at present. They have formed a part of all my past life, and I can trace the evidence of spiritual assistance running like a golden thread through all my intellectual efforts. As I do not desire to practise any deception upon the public, but on the contrary only wish to declare the simple truth, I have published in this volume quite a number of poems, written several years previous to my appearance before the public as a medium or a speaker. Although these were mostly wrought out of my brain by the slow process of thought, yet for some of these, even, I can claim as direct and special an inspiration as for those delivered upon the platform. The first poem in this present work, — "The Prayer of the

Sorrowing," — and that which immediately suc-
ceeds it, — "The Song of Truth," — containing
in itself an answer to the Prayer, were given
to me under peculiar circumstances.   The first
was the language of my own soul, intensified
by an occasion of great mental anguish.   The
second, following directly upon it, was an illumination of my entire being, when I seemed to
have wept away the scales from my eyes, and
"by the deep conflict of my soul in prayer,"
to have broken the fetters of my mortality, and
stepped forth into that freedom whereby I
stood face to face with the ministering spirits,
and heard that "Song of Truth" sounding
through the universe.   I have only known but
few such visitations in my lifetime, but when
they have come, I have felt that I have taken
a free, deep breath of celestial air, and caught a
glimpse of the Realities of Things.   As an im-
mediate consequence, my spirit has become
braver and stronger, and long after my inward vision was closed, the cheering light of

that blessed revelation has lingered in my heart.

Another poem, which bore evidence to me of an inspiration acting upon me, and external to myself, was the "Song of the North," relating to the fate of Sir John Franklin and his men. I was desired to write an illustration for a plate, about to appear in the " Lily of the Valley," an Annual published by J. M. Usher, of Cornhill, Boston. I endeavored to do so, but day after day passed by and my labor was in vain, for not one acceptable idea would suggest itself. The publisher sent for the article, but it was not in being. One day, however, I was seized with an indefinable uneasiness. I wandered up and down through the house and garden, till finally the idea of what I was to do became clearly defined; then, with my paper and pencil, I hastened to a quiet corner in the attic, where nearly all my poems had been written, and there I wrote the Song of the North — so rapidly, that it was scarce legi-

ble, and I was obliged to copy it at once, lest
I should lose the connection. The next day it
seemed as foreign and strange to me as it would
to any one who had never seen it. At the time
this was written (in April, 1853) strong hopes
were entertained of the discovery of Franklin
and his men, together with their safe return ;
therefore I hesitated to make public that which
seemed a decided affirmation to the contrary.
Nevertheless, so strong were my convictions
as to the truth of the poem, that I allowed it
to be published. Later revelations concerning
the fate of that brave adventurer and his companions gave to the poem somewhat of the
character of a prophecy.

How far I have ever written, independent
of these higher influences, I cannot say ; I only
know that all the poems under my own name
have come from the deep places of my " Inner
Life ; " and in that self-same sacred retreat —
which I have entered either by the intense con-
centration of all my intellectual powers, or a

passive surrender to the inspirations that moved
upon me — I have held conscious communion
with disembodied spirits. At such times it has
been said I was " entranced ; " and although that
term does not exactly express my idea, perhaps
it is the best which can yet be found in our
language. The avenues of external sense, if
not entirely closed, were at least disused, in
order that the spiritual perceptions might be
quickened to the required degree, and also that
the world of causes, of which earth and its experiences are but the passing effects, might be
disclosed to my vision. Certain it is that a
physical change took place, affecting both my
breathing and circulation, and my clairvoyant
powers were so strengthened that I could dimly
perceive external objects from the frontal por-
tion of my brain, even with my eyes closed and
bandaged ; also, in that state, any excess of light
was far more painful than under ordinary conditions. If the communications given through my
instrumentality have been weak, erroneous, and

imperfect, it is no fault of my spirit-teachers, but arises rather from my own inability to understand or clearly express what was communicated to me.

In relation to the poems given under direct spirit-influence I would say, that there has been a mistake existing in many minds concerning them, which I take the present opportunity, as far as possible, to correct. They were not like lightning flashes, coming unheralded, and vanishing without leaving a trace behind. Several days before they were given, I would receive intimations of them. Oftentimes, and particularly under the influence of Poe, I would awake in the night from a deep slumber, and detached fragments of those poems would be floating through my mind, though in a few moments after they would vanish like a dream. I have sometimes awakened myself by repeating them aloud. I have been informed, also, by these influences, that all their poems are as complete and finished in spirit-life as they are in this, and the only reason why they cannot be repeated again and again is because of the difficulty of bringing a human organism always into the same state of exaltation — a state in which mediums readily receive inspiration, and render the poems with the least interference of their own intellect.

Among these spiritual poems will be found two purporting to come from Shakspeare. This influence seemed to overwhelm and crush me. I was afraid, and shrank from it. Only those two poems were given, and then the attempt was not repeated. I do not think that the poems in themselves come up to the productions of his master mind. They are only intimations of what might have been, if he had had a stronger and more effectual instrument upon which to pour his inspirations. I have no doubt that time will yet furnish one upon whom his mantle will fall; but I can only say that his power was mightier than I could bear. As I have regarded him spiritually, he seems to be a majestic intellect, but one that overawes rather than attracts me; and my conclusion has been, that while in the flesh, although he was of himself a mighty mind, yet still he spake wiser than he knew, being moved upon by those superior powers who choose men for their mouth-pieces, and oblige them to speak startling words into the dull ear of the times. As all Nature is . a manifestation of Deity, so all Humanity is a manifestation of mind, — differing, however, in degrees of development, — and one body serves as an instrument to effect the purposes of many minds. This is illustrated in the pursuits and employments of ordinary life, and has a far deeper significance when taken in connection with the invisible world.

The influence of Burns was pleasant, easy, and exhilarating, and left me in a cheerful mood. As a spirit, he seemed to be genial and kindly, with a clear perception and earnest love of simple truth, and at the same time a good-natured contempt for all shams, mere forms, and solemn mockeries. This was the way in which

he impressed me, and I felt much more bene-
fited than burdened by his presence.

The first poem delivered by Poe, came to me
far more unexpectedly than any other. By re-
ferring to the introductory remarks, copied from
the " Springfield Republican," it will be seen
that the supposition is presented, that 1, or
" the one who wrote the poem," must have been
very familiar with the writings of Poe. As no
one wrote the poem for me, consequently I am
the only one who can answer to the supposition ;
and I can say, most conscientiously, that previous to that time I had never read, to my
knowledge, any of his poems, save " The Raven,"
and I had not seen that for several years. Indeed, I may well say in this connection, that
I have read, comparatively speaking, very
little poetry in the course of my life, and
have never made the style of any author a
study. The influence of Poe was neither pleasant nor easy. I can only describe it as a
species of mental intoxication. I was tortured

with a feeling of great restlessness and irritability, and strange, incongruous images crowded my brain. Some were bewildering and dazzling as the sun, others dark and repulsive. Under his influence, particularly, I suffered the greatest exhaustion of vital energy, so much so, that after giving one of his poems, I was usually quite ill for several days.

But from his first poem to the last, — " The Farewell to Earth," — was a marked, and rapid change. It would seem as though, in that higher life, where the opportunities for spiritual development far transcend those of earth, that by his quick and active perceptions he had seized upon the Divine Idea which was endeavoring to find expression through his life, both in Time and Eternity; and that from the moment this became apparent, with a volcanic energy, with the battle-strokes of a true hero, he had overthrown every obstacle, and hewn a way through

every barrier that impeded the free out-
growth and manifestation of his diviner self.
His "Farewell" is not a mere poem of the
imagination. It is a record of facts. I can
clearly perceive, as his spirit has been revealed to me, that there was a deep significance in his words, when he said, —

> "I will sunder, and forever,
> Every tie of *human passion* that can bind my soul to Earth —
> Every *slavish* tie that binds me to the things of little worth."

As he last appeared to me, he was full
of majesty and strength, self-poised and
calm, and it would seem by the expression
of his countenance, radiant with victory, that
the reward promised to "him that over-
cometh," had been made his sure possession.
Around his brow, as a spiritual emblem,
was an olive-wreath, whose leaves glowed
like fire. He stood upon the side of a
mountain, which was white and glittering like
crystal, and the full tide of inspiration to

which he gave utterance could not be comprehended in human speech. That last "Farewell," as it found expression through my weak lips, was but the faintest possible echo of that most musical and majestic lyric which thrilled the harp-strings of my being. In order to be fully realized and understood, the soul must be transported to that sphere of spiritual *perceptions*, where there is no *audible* "speech nor language," and where the "voice is not *heard*."

Obedient to the call of the Angels, he has "gone up higher" in the ways of Eternal Progress; and though, because of this change, he may no longer manifest himself as he *was*, yet doubtless as he *is*, he will yet be felt as a Presence and a Power in the "Heaven" of many a human heart. Upon earth he was a meteor light, flashing with a startling brilliancy across the intellectual firmament; but now he is a star of ever-increasing magnitude, which has at length

gravitated to its own place among the celestial spheres.

In saying thus much, I cannot so play
the coward to my spiritual convictions as to
offer the slightest apology for any ideas I
may have advanced contrary to popular prej-
udices or time-honored opinions. O, thought-
ful reader ! if I have offended thee, say
simply that these are *my* convictions and
not *yours*, and do not fear for the result;
for in whatsoever I purpose or perform,
I "can do nothing against the Truth — only
for it." I do not indulge in the conceit
that this little work has any important mission to perform, or that it will cause any
commotion in the literary world. But I
have felt, as one by one these poems have
been wrought out — by general or special
inspiration — from my "Inner Life," that in
this matter I had a work, simple though
it might be, to do, and my soul was sorely
"straitened till it was accomplished."

c

As some of these poems, appearing at various times, have been severely criticized in the past, so I would say now, that if any there should be, who, through biogtry, or prejudice, or a desire to display their superior wisdom, should choose to criticize them in their present form — to such I shall make no answer. But to all those earnest and inquiring souls, who feel that in such experiences as I have described, or in the resources from which my soul has drawn its supply, there is aught that is attractive or desirable to them, I would say, "God speed you in your search for Truth!" At the same time let me assure you, that in the depths of your own Inner Life there is a fountain of inspiration and wisdom, which, if sought aright, will yield you more abundant satisfaction than any simple cup of the living water which I, or any other individual, can place to your lips. There are invisible teachers around you, the hem of

whose garments I am unworthy to touch.
" The words that they speak unto you —
they are Spirit and they are Life." " In
order to *know* more you must *be* more."
Faith strikes its roots deep in the spirit,
and often Intuition is a safer guide than
Reason. When a man, by constant practice,
has so quickened his spiritual perceptions
that he can receive conscious impressions
from his invisible attendants, he will never
be without counsellors.

> " Let Faith be given
> To the still tones that oft our being waken —
> They are of Heaven."

The Spirit-World is not so distant as it
seems, and the veil of Materiality which
hides it from our view, by hopeful and un-
tiring aspiration can be rent in twain. We
only need listen earnestly and attentively,
and we shall soon learn to keep step in
the grand march of Life to the music of

the upper spheres.   As a popular author
has beautifully said, " Silence is vocal, if
we listen well."   With a sublime accord, the
great anthem of the Infinite "rolls and re-
sounds" through the Universe, and whosoever
will, can listen to that harmony, till all
special and particular discords shall die out
from the "Inner Life," and the Heaven of
the celestial intelligences shall blend with the
"Heaven within," in perfect unison !

POEMS

THE INNER LIFE

PART I.

1   (1)

POEMS

FROM THE INNER LIFE.

.

—

THE PRAYER OF THE SORROWING.

" And there appeared an angel unto him from heaven strengthening him."

God! hear my prayer!
Thou who hast poured the essence of thy life
  Into this urn, this feeble urn of clay;
Thou who amid the tempest's gloom and strife
  Art the lone star that guides me on my way;
When my crushed heart, by constant striving torn,
  Flies shuddering from its own impurity,
And my faint spirit, by its sorrows worn,
  Turns with a cry of anguish unto thee —
      Hear me, O God! my God!

(3)

O, this strange mingling in of Life and Death,
    Of Soul and Substance! Let me comprehend
The hidden secret of life's fleeting breath,
    My being's destiny, its aim and end.
Show me the impetus that urged me forth, .
    Upon my lone and burning pathway driven;
The secret force that binds me down to earth,
    While my sad spirit yearns for home and heaven —
       Hear me, O God! my God!

The ruby life-drops from my heart are wrung,
    By the deep conflict of my soul in prayer;
The words lie burning on my feeble tongue;
    Aid me, O Father! let me not despair.
Save, Lord! I perish! Save me, ere I die!
    My rebel spirit mocks at thy control —
The raging billows rise to drown my cry;
    The floods of anguish overwhelm my soul —
       Hear me, O God! my God!

Peace! peace! O, wilful, wayward heart, be still!
    For, lo! the messenger of God is near;
Bow down submissive to the Father's will,
    In "perfect love" that "casteth out all fear."

O, pitying Spirit from the home above!

  No longer shall my chastened heart rebel;

Fold me, O fold me in thine arms of love!

  I know my Father "doeth all things well;"

I will not doubt his changeless love again.

        Amen! My heart repeats, Amen!

      1*

THE SONG OF TRUTH.

FROM the unseen throne of the Great Unknown,
   From the Soul of All, I came;
Not with the rock of the earthquake's shock,
   And not with the wasting flame.
But silent and deep is my onward sweep,
   Through the depths of the boundless sky;
I stand sublime, through the lapse of time,
   And where God is, there am I.

In the early years, when the youthful spheres,
   From the depths of Chaos sprung,
When the heavens grew bright with the new-born
      light,
   And the stars in chorus sung —
To that holy sound, through the space profound,
   'Mid their glittering ranks I trod;

For I am a part of the Central Heart,
  Co-equal and one with God.

The world is my child. Though wilful and wild,
  Yet I know that she loves me still,
For she thinks I fled with her holy dead,
  Because of her stubborn will;
And she weeps at night, when the angels light
  Their watch-fires over the sky,
Like a maid o'er the grave of her loved and brave;
  But the Truth can never die.

One by one, like sparks *from* the sun,
  I have counted the souls that came
From the hand Divine; — all, all are mine,
  And I call them by my name.
One by one, like sparks *to* the sun,
  I shall see them all return;
Though tempest-tost, yet they are not lost,
  And not one shall cease to burn.

I only speak to the lowly and meek,
  To the simple and child-like heart,

But I leave the proud to their glittering shroud,
    And the tricks of their cunning art.
Like a white-winged dove from the home of love,
    Through the airy space untrod,
I come at the cry which is heard on high, —
    "Hear me, O God! my God!"

THE EMBARKATION.

"So they left that goodly and pleasant city, which had been their resting-place near twelve years. But they knew they were *pilgrims*, and looked not much to those things; but lifted their eyes to heaven, their dearest country, and quieted their spirits." — *E. Winslow.*

THE band of Pilgrim exiles in tearful silence stood,
While thus outspake, in parting, John Robinson
      the good:
"Fare thee well, my brave Miles Standish! thou
      hast a trusty sword,
But not with carnal weapons shalt thou glorify
      the Lord.
Fare thee well, good Elder Brewster! thou art a
      man of prayer;
Commend the flock I give thee to the holy Shep-
      herd's care.
And thou, belovéd Carver, what shall I say to
      thee?

I have need, in this my sorrow, that thou shouldst
    comfort me.

In the furnace of affliction must all be sharply
    tried;

But nought prevails against us, if the Lord be on
    our side.

Farewell, farewell, my people!—go, and stay not
    the hand,

But precious seed of Freedom sow ye broadcast
    through the land.

Ye may scatter it in sorrow, and water it with
    tears,

But rejoice for those who gather the fruit in after
    years;

Ay! rejoice that ye may leave them an altar unto
    God,

On the holy soil of Freedom, where no tyrant's foot
    hath trod.

All honor to our sovereign, his majesty King James,

But the King of kings above us the highest homage
    claims."

Upon the deck together they knelt them down
    and prayed,
The husband and the father, the matron and the
    maid;
The broad blue heavens above them, bright with
    the summer's glow,
And the wide, wide waste of waters, with its treach-
    erous waves below;
Around, the loved and cherished, whom they should
    see no more,
And the dark, uncertain future stretching dimly on
    before.
O, well might Edward Winslow look sadly on his
    bride!
O, well might fair Rose Standish press to her chief-
    tain's side!
For with crucified affections they bowed the knee in
    prayer,
And besought that God would aid them to suffer
    and to bear;
To bear the cross of sorrow — a broader shield of
    love
Than the Royal Cross of England, that proudly
    waved above.

The balmy winds of summer swept o'er the glit-
    tering seas;
It brought the sign of parting — the white sails met
    the breeze;
One farewell gush of sorrow, one prayerful blessing
    more,
And the bark that bore the exiles glided slowly
    from the shore.
"Thus they left that goodly city," o'er stormy seas
    to roam;
"But they knew that they were pilgrims," and this
    world was not their home.

There is a God in heaven, whose purpose none may
    tell;
There is a God in heaven, who doeth all things
    well:
And thus an infant nation was cradled on the
    deep,
While hosts of holy angels were set to guard its
    sleep;
No seer, no priest, or prophet, read its horoscope at
    birth,
No bard in solemn saga sung its destiny to earth,

But slowly, — slowly, — slowly as the acorn from
    the sod,
It grew in strength and grandeur, and spread its
    arms abroad;
The eyes of distant nations turned towards that
    goodly tree,
And they saw how fair and pleasant were the fruits
    of Liberty!
Like earth's convulsive motion before the earth-
    quake's shock,
Like the foaming of the ocean around old Plymouth
    Rock,
So the deathless love of Freedom — the majesty
    of Right —
In all kindred, and all nations, is rising in its might;
And words of solemn warning come from the hon-
    ored dead —
"Woe, woe to the oppressor if righteous blood be
    shed!
Rush not blindly on the future! heed the lessons
    of the past!
For the feeble and the faithful are the conquerors at
    last."

KEPLER'S VISION.

"How grand the spectacle of a mind thus restless — thirsting
with unquenchable appetite after beauty and harmony! Never was
there a finer example of a spirit too vast to be satiated with the few
truths around it, or one that more emphatically foreboded a necessary immortality." — *Prof. R. P. Nichol.*

Upon the clear, bright, northern sky,
    Aurora's rainbow arches gleamed,
While, from their radiant source on high,
    The countless host of evening beamed;
Each moving in its path of light —
    Those paths by Science then untrod —
The silent guardians of the night,
    The watchers by the throne of God.

Far up above the gloomy wood, —
    The wavy, murmuring wood of pine, —
Upon the mountain side, there stood
    A worshipper at Nature's shrine.

His spirit, like a breathing lyre,
　At each celestial touch awoke,
And burning with a sacred fire,
　His voice the solemn silence broke.

"O, glittering host! O, golden line!
　I would I had an angel's ken,
Your deepest secrets to divine,
　And read your mysteries to men.
The glorious truth is in my soul,
　The solemn witness in my heart—
Although ye move as one great whole,
　Each bears his own appointed part."

＊　　＊　　＊　　＊　　＊　　＊

He slept. No! in a blissful trance
　The feebler powers of Nature lay,
While upward, o'er the vast expanse,
　His eager spirit swept away,—
Away into those fields of light,
　By human footsteps unexplored;
Order and beauty met his sight—
　He saw, he wondered, and adored!

And o'er the vast area of space,
    And through the height and depth profound,
Each starless void and shining place
    Was filled with harmony of sound.
Now, swelling like the voice of seas,
    With the full, rushing tide of years,
Then, sighing like an evening breeze,
    It died among the distant spheres.

Rich goblets filled with "Samian wine,"
    Or "Life's elixir, sparkling high,"
Could not impart such joy divine
    As that full chorus of the sky.
He might have heard the Orphean lute,
    Or caught the sound of Memnon's lyre,
And yet his lips could still be mute,
    Nor feel one spark of kindred fire.

But now, o'er ravished soul and sense,
    Such floods of living music broke,
That, filled with rapture too intense,
    His disenchanted spirit woke.
Awoke! but not to lose the sound,
    The echo of that holy song;

He breathed it to the world around,
 And others bore the strain along.

O, unto few the power is given
 To pass beyond the bounds of Time,
And lift the radiant veil of Heaven,
 To view her mysteries sublime.
Yet Thou, in whose majestic light
 The Source of Knowledge lies concealed,
Prepare us to receive aright
 The truths that yet shall be revealed.

2 *

LOVE AND LATIN.

Amo — amare — amavi — amatum.*

DEAR girls, never marry for knowledge,
　(Though that should of course form a part,)
For often the head, in a college,
　Gets wise at the cost of the heart.
Let me tell you a fact that is real —
　I once had a beau in my youth,
My brightest and best *"beau ideal"*
　Of manliness, goodness, and truth.

O, he talked of the Greeks and the Romans,
　Of Normans, and Saxons, and Celts,
And he quoted from Virgil, and Homer,
　And Plato, and —— somebody else.
And he told me his deathless affection,
　By means of a thousand strange herbs,

---

* Principal parts of the Latin verb *amo* — I love.

With numberless words in connection,
   Derived from the roots of Greek verbs.

One night, as a sly innuendo,
   When Nature was mantled in snow,
He wrote in the frost on the window,
   A sweet word in Latin — "amo."
O, it needed no words for expression,
   For that I had long understood;
But there was his written confession —
   Present tense and indicative mood.

But O, how man's passion will vary!
   For scarcely a year had passed by,
When he changed the "amo" to "amare,"
   But instead of an "e" was a "y."
Yes, a Mary had certainly taken
   The heart once so fondly my own,
And I, the rejected, forsaken,
   Was left to reflection alone.

Since then I've a horror of Latin,
   And students uncommonly smart;

True love, one should always put that in,
  To balance the head by the heart.
To be a fine scholar and linguist
  Is much to one's credit, I know,
But "I love" should be said in plain English,
  And not with a Latin "amo."

THE FATE OF SIR JOHN FRANKLIN.

" In March, of 1851, says the Cleveland Herald, several months before the arrival of Dr. Rae, with his news of the probable death of the brave Sir John Franklin and his faithful comrades, we copied from the Lily of the Valley for 1854, a beautiful poem by Miss Lizzie Doten, in reference to these adventurers. The verses are touching and solemn as the sound of a passing bell, and appear *almost prophetic* of the news that afterwards came. 'The Song of the North' again becomes deeply interesting as connected with the thrilling account brought home by the Fox — the last vessel sent in search of the lost adventurers to the icy North, and the last that will now ever be sent on such an expedition." — *Buffalo Daily Republic.*

SONG OF THE NORTH.

"Away, away!" cried the stout Sir John,
  " While the blossoms are on the trees,
For the summer is short, and the times speeds on
  As we sail for the northern seas.
Ho! gallant Crozier, and brave Fitz James!
  We will startle the world, I trow,
When we find a way through the Northern seas
  That never was found till now!

A good stout ship is the ' Erebus,'
   As ever unfurled a sail,
And the 'Terror' will match with as brave a one
   As ever outrode a gale."

So they bade farewell to their pleasant homes,
   To the hills and the valleys green,
With three hearty cheers for their native isle,
   And three for the English Queen.
They sped them away, beyond cape and bay,
   Where the day and the night are one —
Where the hissing light in the heavens grew bright,
   And flamed like a midnight sun.
There was nought below, save the fields of snow,
   That stretched to the icy pole;
And the Esquimaux, in his strange canoe,
   Was the only living soul!

Along the coast, like a giant host,
   The glittering icebergs frowned,
Or they met on the main, like a battle plain,
   And crashed with a fearful sound!
The seal and the bear, with a curious stare,
   Looked down from the frozen heights,

And the stars in the skies, with their great, wild eyes,
    Peered out from the Northern Lights.
The gallant Crozier, and brave Fitz James,
    And even the stout Sir John,
Felt a doubt, like a chill, through their warm
        hearts thrill,
    As they urged the good ships on.

They sped them away, beyond cape and bay,
    Where even the tear-drops freeze,
But no way was found, by a strait or sound,
    To sail through the Northern seas;
They sped them away, beyond cape and bay,
    And they sought, but they sought in vain,
For no way was found, through the ice around,
    To return to their homes again.
Then the wild waves rose, and the waters froze,
    Till they closed like a prison wall;
And the icebergs stood in the sullen flood,
    Like their jailers, grim and tall.
O God! O God!—it was hard to die
    In that prison house of ice!
For what was fame, or a mighty name,
    When life was the fearful price?

The gallant Crozier, and brave Fitz James,
   And even the stout Sir John,
Had a secret dread, and their hopes all fled,
   As the weeks and the months passed on.
Then the Ice King came, with his eyes of flame,
   And looked on that fated crew;
His chilling breath was as cold as death,
   And it pierced their warm hearts through!
A heavy sleep, that was dark and deep,
   Came over their weary eyes,
And they dreamed strange dreams of the hills and
      streams,
   And the blue of their native skies.

The Christmas chimes, of the good old times,
   Were heard in each dying ear,
And the dancing feet, and the voices sweet
   Of their wives and their children dear!
But it faded away — away — away!
   Like a sound on a distant shore,
And deeper and deeper grew the sleep,
   Till they slept to wake no more.

O, the sailor's wife, and the sailor's child,
   They will weep, and watch, and pray;

And the Lady Jane, she will hope in vain,
  As the long years pass away!
The gallant Crozier, and brave Fitz James,
  And the good Sir John have found
An open way, to a quiet bay,
  And a port where we all are bound!
Let the waters roar on the ice-bound shore,
  That circles the frozen pole;
But there is no sleep, and no grave so deep,
  That can hold a human soul.

3

THE BURIAL OF WEBSTER.

Low and solemn be the requiem above the nation's
    dead;
Let fervent prayers be uttered, and farewell bless-
    ings said!
Close by the sheltering homestead, beneath the
    household tree,
Where oft his footsteps lingered, here let the part-
    ing be!
Draw near in solemn silence, with slow and meas-
    ured tread;
Come with the brow uncovered, and gaze upon the
    dead!
How like a fallen hero, in silent rest he lies!
With the seal of Death upon him, and its dimness
    in his eyes!
Speak! but there comes no answer.   That voice
    of power is still

Which woke the slumbering Senate as with a
    giant's will! —
That voice, which rang so proudly back from the
    echoing walls,
In court and civic council, and legislative halls;
Which summoned back those spirits, who long were
    mute and still, —
The Pilgrim sires of Plymouth — the dead of
    Bunker Hill, —
And in their silent presence gave to the past a
    tongue
Like that which roused the nations when Freedom's
    war-cry rung.
But now, the roar of cannon, the thunder of the
    deep,
The battle-shock of earthquakes, cannot wake him
    from his sleep!
The foot that trod so proudly upon the earth's green
    sod,
The manly form, created in the image of its God,
The brow, where mental greatness had set her
    noblest seal,
The lip, whence thoughts were uttered like shafts
    of polished steel, —

All, all of these shall moulder back to their parent
    earth,
Back to the silent bosom from whence they sprang
    to birth!
The *man*, — the *living Webster*, — passed with a
    fleeting breath!
Alas, for *human* greatness! — the end thereof is
    death!
O! what is earthly glory? Ask Cæsar, when he
    fell
At the base of Pompey's statue, slain by those he
    loved too well;
Ask the Carthaginian hero, who kept his fearful
    vow;
Ask Napoleon in his exile; ask the dead before
    ye now; —
And one answer, and one only, in the light of truth
    is given:
"Man's highest earthly glory is to do the will of
    Heaven;
To rise and battle bravely, with dauntless moral
    might,
In the holy cause of Freedom, and the triumph of
    the Right!"

For by this simple standard shall all at last be
    tried,
And not by earthly glory, or works of human pride.

O Webster! thou wast mighty among thy fellow-
    men;
And he who seeks to judge thee must be what
    thou hast been; —
Must feel thine aspirations for higher aims in
    life,
And know the stern temptations that urged thee
    in the strife;
Must let his heart flow largely from out its narrow
    span,
And meet thee freely, fairly, as man should meet
    with man.
What was lost, and what resisted, is known to
    One alone:
Then let him who stands here guiltless "be first
    to cast a stone"!

Farewell! We give, with mourning, back to thy
    mother Earth
The robes thy soul rejected at its celestial birth!

3 *

A mightier one and stronger may stand where thou
    wast tried,
Yet he shall be the wiser that thou hast lived and
    died;
Thy greatness be his glory, thine errors let him
    shun,
And let him finish nobly what thou hast left un-
    done.

Farewell! The granite mountains, the hill-side, and
    the sea,
Thy harvest-fields and orchards, will all lament for
    thee!
Farewell! A mighty nation awards thee deathless
    fame,
And future generations shall honor WEBSTER's
    name!

THE PARTING OF SIGURD AND GERDA.

"He is a strong, proud man, such as a woman might, with pride, call her partner — 'if only — O! if he would but understand her nature, and allow it to be worth something.'" — *See Miss Bremer's "Brothers and Sisters."*

SHE stood beneath the moonlight pale,
    With calm, uplifted eye,
While all her being, weak and frail,
    Thrilled with her purpose high;
For she, the long affianced bride,
    Must seal the fount of tears,
And break, with woman's lofty pride,
    The plighted faith of years.

Ay! she had loved as in a dream,
    And woke, at length, to find
How coldly on her spirit gleamed
    The dazzling light of mind.
For little was the true, deep love

Of that pure spirit known
To him, the cold, the selfish one,
Who claimed her as his own.

And what to him were all her dreams
Of purer, holier life?
Such idle fancies ill became
A meek, submissive wife.
And what were all her yearnings high
For God and " Fatherland "
But vain chimeras, lofty flights,
While Sigurd held her hand?

And then uprose the bitter thought,
" Why bow to his control?
Why sacrifice, before his pride,
The freedom of my soul?
Better to break the golden chain,
And live and love apart,
Than feel the galling, grinding links
Wearing upon my heart."

He came, — and, with a soft, low voice,
In the pale gleaming light,

She laid her gentle hand in his —
  "Sigurd, we part to-night.
Long have these bitter words been kept
  Within this heart of mine,
And often have I lonely wept, —
  I never can be thine."

Proudly, with folded arms he stood,
  And cold, sarcastic smile —
"Ha! this is but a wayward mood,
  An artful woman's wile.
But this I know: so long — so long
  I've held thee to thy vow,
That I have made the bond too strong
  For thee to break it now."

"You know me not; — my lofty pride
  Was hidden from your eyes;
But you have crushed it down so low
  It gives me strength to rise.
O! all my bitter, burning thoughts
  I may not, dare not tell!
Sigurd, my loved — *forever* loved!
  Farewell! once more, farewell!"

One moment, and those loving arms
  Were gently round him thrown;
One moment, and those quivering lips
  Pressed lightly to his own:
And then he stood alone! *alone!*
  With eyes too proud for tears;
Yet o'er his stern, cold heart was thrown
  The burning blight of years.

O man! so God-like in thy strength,
  Preëminent in mind,
Seek not with these high gifts alone,
  A woman's heart to bind.
For, timid as a shrinking fawn,
  Yet faithful as a dove,
She clings through life and death to thee,
  Won by thine *earnest love.*

THE MEETING OF SIGURD AND GERDA.

"And beautiful now stood they there, man and woman ; no longer pale ; eye to eye, hand to hand, as equals, — as partners in the light of heaven." — *See Miss Bremer's "Brothers and Sisters."*

"O, EARLY love ! O, early love !
    Why does this memory haunt me yet ?
Peace ! I invoke thee from above, —
    I cannot, though I would, forget.
How have I strove, with prayers and tears,
    To quench this wasting passion-flame !
But after long, long, weary years,
    It burns within my heart the same."

She wept — poor, sorrowing Gerda wept,
    In the dark pine-wood wandering lone,
While cold the night-winds past her swept,
    And bright the stars above her shone.
Poor, suffering dove ! her song was hushed,

The blithesome song of other days,
    Yet, O ! when such true hearts are crushed,
    They breathe their holiest, sweetest lays.

A step was heard.   Her heart beat high ;
    Through the dim shadows of the wood
She glanced with quick and anxious eye —
    Lo ! Sigurd by her stood ; —
And as the moon's pale, quivering rays
    Stole through that lonely place,
He stood, with calm, impassioned gaze
    Fixed on her tearful face.

" Gerda," he said, " I come to speak
    A long, a last farewell ;
Some distant land and home I seek,
    Far, far from thee to dwell.
O, since I lost thee, gentle one,
    My truest and my best,
I have rushed madly, blindly on,
    Nor dared to think of rest.

"The night that spreads her starry wing
    Beyond the Northern Sea,

Does not a deeper darkness bring
 Than that which rests on me.
Yet, no! I will not ask thy tears
 For my deep tale of woe;
Forgetfulness will come with years;
 Gerda — my love — I go!"

" Stay! Sigurd, stay! O, why depart?
 See, at *thy feet* I bow;
O, cherished idol of my heart,
 Reject — reject *me* now!"
But not upon the cold, damp ground,
 Her bended knee she pressed;
Upheld, and firmly clasped around,
 She wept upon his breast.

" Reject thee? No! When earth rejects
 The sunshine's summer glow,
When Heaven one suppliant's prayer neglects,
 Then will I bid *thee* go.
And, by the watching stars above,
 And by all things divine,
I swear to cherish and to love
 This heart that beats to mine!"

O, holy sense of wrongs forgot,
  And injuries forgiven !
The human heart that feels thee not,
  Knows not the peace of Heaven.
Ye blessèd spirits from above,
  Who guide us while we live,
O, teach us also how to love,
  And freely to forgive.

POEMS

FROM

THE INNER LIFE.

PART II.

(69)

THE succeeding poems were given under direct spirit influence before public audiences. For many of them I could not obtain the authorship, but for such as I could, the names are given.

POEMS

FROM THE INNER LIFE.

THE SPIRIT-CHILD.

BY "JENNIE."

O, THOU holy Heaven above us!
O, ye angel hosts who love us!
Ye alone know how to prove us
    By the discipline of life —
That we faint not in endeavor,
But with cheerful courage ever
    Rise victorious in the strife.

O, my sister! O, my brother
I was once a mortal mother;

4*   (41)

One sweet blossom, and no other,
    Bloomed upon the household tree:
Very fragile, very tender,
Very beautiful and slender —
    He was dear as life to me.

All the spring-time's fresh unfolding,
All of Art's exquisite moulding,
All that thrills one in beholding,
    Centred in that fair young face;
While an angel-tempered gladness,
Almost blending into sadness,
    Filled him with a nameless grace.

And I loved him without measure;
O, a ceaseless fount of pleasure
Found I in that little treasure!
    And my heart grew good and great,
As I thanked the God of Heaven
That this precious one was given
    Thus to cheer my low estate.

But, with all my prayers ascending,
I could hear a low voice blending,

Like some benison descending,
    Saying, "Place thy hopes above;
For the test of all affection
Is the full and free rejection
    Of all selfishness in love."

Then I felt a sad foreboding,
All my soul to anguish goading,
All my inward peace corroding;
    And my rebel heart begun,
Crying wildly, that I would not
Yield my precious one — I could not
    Say, "Thy will, not mine, be done."

Spring-time came with genial showers,
Bursting buds and opening flowers,
Singing birds and sunny hours,
    Filling heaven and earth with light.
But the Summer — fair deceiver! —
Came with pestilence and fever,
    Came my little bud to blight.

O'er my threshold silent stealing,
Chilling every sense and feeling,

All the fount of grief unsealing,
    Came the great white angel, Death ;
And my flower upon my bosom
Withered, like an early blossom
    Stricken by the north wind's breath.

And I saw him weakly lying,
Heard his parched lips faintly sighing,
Knew that he was dying — *dying!*
    And my love was vain to save!
All my wild, impassioned pleading,
All my fervent interceding,
    Could not triumph o'er the grave.

Vainly did I crave permission,
That my anxious, tearful vision,
Might behold the land Elysian —
    Forth into the unknown dark,
On that broad, mysterious river,
Did the hand of God, the Giver,
    Launch that little, fragile bark.

Then my brain grew wild to madness,
Changing to a sullen sadness,

Tempered by no ray of gladness;
 And I cursed the God above,
That, with Heaven all full of angels,
Sounding forth their glad evangels,
 He should take my little dove.

Then my eyelids knew no sleeping:
Once my midnight watch while keeping,
I had wept beyond all weeping, —
 Suddenly there seemed to fall
From my spiritual being,
From my inward sense of seeing,
 Scales, as from the eyes of Paul.

Heavenly gales were round me playing,
Angel hands my soul were staying,
And I heard a clear voice saying,
 "Come up hither, — come and see!
O, thou sorrow-stricken mother!
Unto thee, as to none other,
 Heaven unfolds her mystery."

God's own Spirit seemed to move me,
All the Heaven grew bright above me,

All the angels seemed to love me, —
    Waved their white hands as they smiled;
And one, fair as Summer moonlight,
Crowned with starry gems of midnight,
    Brought to me my angel child.

Like a flower in sunshine blowing,
Cheeks, and lips, and eyes were glowing, —
I could see that he was growing
    Fairer than the things of earth.
"Thou mayst take him," said the spirit,
"Back to earth, there to inherit
    All the woes of mortal birth."

I had need of no advising;
In divinest strength arising,
All my selfishness despising, —
    "Nay!" I cried; "now first I know
What it is to be a mother,
To give being to another
    Living soul, for joy or woe.

"Keep him in these heavenly places,
Fold him in your pure embraces,

Teach him the divinest graces:
　　I return to earth again ;
Not to sit and weep supinely,
But to live and love divinely."
　　And the angels said, "Amen!"

O thou holy Heaven above us!
O ye angel hosts who love us!
Ye alone know how to prove us,
　　By the discipline of life,—
That we faint not in endeavor,
But with cheerful courage ever
　　Rise victorious in the strife.

RECONCILIATION.

God of the Granite and the Rose!
　Soul of the Sparrow and the Bee!
The mighty tide of Being flows
　Through countless channels, Lord, from thee.
It leaps to life in grass and flowers,
　Through every grade of being runs,
Till from Creation's radiant towers
　Its glory flames in stars and suns.

O, ye who sit and gaze on life
　With folded hands and fettered will,
Who only see, amid the strife,
　The dark supremacy of ill, —
Know, that like birds, and streams, and flowers,
　The life that moves you is divine!
Nor time, nor space, nor human powers,
　Your Godlike spirit can confine.

Once, in a form of human mould,
　　Upon this earthly plane I trod;
My faith was weak, my heart was cold,—
　　I had no hope, I knew not God.
Deep from my being's cup I quaffed,
　　With Life's Elixir brimming o'er,
And madly sought to drain the draught,
　　That I might die, to live no more!

There came an angel to my side—
　　Not from the bowers of Paradise—
She was mine own, mine earthly bride,
　　With Heaven's pure sunshine in her eyes.
She wept and prayed, she knew not why—
　　Her Faith, not Reason, soared above:
She talked of God and Heaven—and I—
　　Well—I was happy in *her* love.

Love was my all, my guiding star,
　　And like a wanderer in the night,
I hailed its radiance from afar,
　　Because it shone with *certain* light;
But all those visions, bright and high,
　　Which the pure-hearted only see,

Of God and Immortality,
  Could not reveal their light to me.

At length my precious one, my wife,
  Held on her bosom's sacred shrine
A tender form, — an infant life, —
  The union of her soul and mine.
O God! above that precious child
  First did I breathe thy holy name,
While strong emotions, deep and wild,
  Shook like a reed my manly frame.

I prayed for Heaven's eternal years;
  I prayed for light, that I might see;
And even with stern manhood's tears,
  I prayed for faith, O God, in Thee.
O, this poor world seemed far too small
  To hold the measure of my love!
They were my God, my Heaven, my All —
  My precious wife, my nestling dove.

Ay, then there came a fearful day,
  A day of sorrow and of pain,
When, like a helpless child, I lay,

And fever burned in every vein.
Weeks came and went, they went and came,
　　Till Faith was Fear, and Hope had died,
And I could only breathe the name
　　Of the lone watcher at my side.

With patient love that could not fail,
　　And anxious care that knew no rest,
She sat, like a Madonna, pale,
　　With our sweet infant on her breast.
For *them* I beat Life's stormy wave,
　　And struggled, face to face, with death;
For *them* I tarried from the grave,
　　And firmly held my mortal breath.

But faint and weak at length I lay,
　　While darkness gathered over all —
I felt my pulses fluttering play
　　Like Autumn leaves about to fall.
My poor, tired heart could do no more,
　　But yielded the unequal strife;
Ay, then I prayed, as ne'er before,
　　That I might have Eternal Life.

O God! my sainted mother's face ·
  Gleamed through the deepening shades of
    death,
And from her lips these words of grace
  Fell gently as the evening's breath:
"Child of my love, I gave to earth
  Thy mortal form in grief and pain —
Lo! now, in this, thy second birth,
  I lend my strength to thee again."

That angel-presence stood revealed,
  To her who sat beside my bed;
Our quivering lips Love's compact sealed,
  And one, brief, parting word was said.
Then, leaning like a weary child
  My head upon my mother's breast,
She bore me, changed and reconciled,
  To the fair dwellings of the blest.

But oft at morn, or close of day,
  I feel the love that toward me yearns,
And earthward, o'er the starry way,
  My answering spirit gladly turns.
O Death! O Grave! before Heaven's light

Thy gloomy phantoms quickly fly;
And man shall learn *this* truth aright —
That he must *change*, but shall not *die!*

Shall change, as doth the summer rose,
  The evening light, the closing year;
Shall sink into a sweet repose,
  To waken in a happier sphere; —
Shall fall, as falls the harvest grain —
  The ripened ears of golden corn,
Which yields its life, that yet again,
  Through ceaseless change, it be re-born.

God of the Granite and the Rose!
  Soul of the Sparrow and the Bee!
The mighty tide of Being flows
  Through all thy creatures back to Thee.
Thus round and round the circle runs —
  A mighty sea without a shore —
While men and angels, stars and suns,
  Unite to praise Thee evermore!

5 *

HOPE FOR THE SORROWING.

[A poem delivered at the funeral service of Mr. Henry L. Kingman, of North Bridgewater, Mass., November, 1862.]

YE holy ministers of Love,
  Blest dwellers in the upper spheres,
In vain we fix our gaze above,
  For we are blinded by our tears.
O, tell us to what land unknown
The soul of him we love has flown?

He left us when his manly heart
  With earnest hope was beating high;
Too soon it seemed for us to part;
  Too soon, alas! for him to die.
We have the tenement of clay,
But aye the soul has passed away.

Away, into the unknown dark,
  With fearless heart and steady hand,

He calmly launched his fragile bark,
　To seek the spirits' Father Land.
Say, has he reached some distant shore,
To speak with us or earth no more?

We gaze into unmeasured space,
　And lift our tearful eyes above,
To catch the gleaming of his face,
　Or one light whisper of his love.
O God! O Angels! hear our cry,
Nor let our faith in darkness die!

Hark! for a voice of gentle tone
　The answer to our cry hath given,
Soft as Æolian harpstrings blown,
　Responsive to the breath of even —
"I have not sought a distant shore;
Lo! I am with you — weep no more.

"Ay! Love is stronger far than death,
　And wins the victory o'er the Grave;
Dependent on no mortal breath,
　Its mission is to guide and save.
Above the wrecks of Death and Time,
It triumphs, changeless and sublime.

" Still shall my love its vigils keep,
    True as the needle to the pole,
For Death is not a dreamless sleep,
    Nor is the Grave man's final goal.
The larger growth, — the life divine, —
All that I hoped or wished, are mine."

Blest spirit! we will weep no more,
    But lay our selfishness to rest;
The Providence, which we adore,
    Has ordered all things for the best.
Life's battle fought, the victory won,
To nobler toils pass on! pass on!

COMPENSATION.

OUT in the desolate midnight,
  Out in the cold and rain,
With the bitter, bleak winds of winter
  Driving across the plain —
In the ghastly gloom of the churchyard,
  Crouching behind a stone,
Fleeing from what is called Justice,
  I was safe with the dead alone.

All of the madness and evil
  That into my nature was cast;
All of the demon or devil
  Had filled up its measure at last.
Blood, on my hands, of a brother!
  Blood — an indelible stain!
Burning, and smarting, and eating
  Into my heart and my brain.

In woe and iniquity shapen,
   Conceived by my mother in sin,
Forecast in a soil of pollution,
   Did the life of my being begin.
I chose not the nature within me;
   I was fated and fashioned by birth;
Forordained to the darkness and evil,
   The sins and the sorrows of earth!

The World was my foe ere it knew me;
   It scattered its snares in my path:
Like a serpent, it charmed and it drew me,
   Then met me with judgment and wrath!
I saw that the strong crushed the weaker,
   That wickedness won in the strife,
And the greatest of crimes and of curses
   Was the lot of a beggar in life!

E'en the arm of God's mercy seemed shortene',
   For all that could gladden or save;
The child of my love, and its mother,
   Were laid in the pitiless grave!
Then, weakened and wasted by hunger —
   Ay, famished without and within —

All homeless, and hopeless, and friendless,
   O, what was there left me but sin?

I met in the wood-path a lordling,
   Arrayed in his garments of pride,
And, like Moses who slew the Egyptian,
   I smote him so sore that he died!
O, the blood on my hands and my garments!
   O, the terrible face of the dead!
His gold could not tempt me to linger —
   I turned in my horror, and fled!

I fled, but a terrible phantom
   Pursued like a demon of wrath;
In the forest, the field, or the churchyard,
   Its footsteps were close on my path;
And there, on the grave of my loved ones,
   As freezing and famished I lay,
I was seized by the human avenger,
   And borne to the judgment away!

O, the prison! the sentence! the gallows!
   That last fearful struggle for breath!

The rush, and the roar, and confusion,
    The depth and the darkness of death!
O man! I have sinned and have suffered;
    The climax of evil is past;
But the justice of time may determine
    That *you* were more guilty at last!

Then long did I struggle with phantoms,
    And wandered in darkness and night,
Till there came to my soul, in its prison,
    The form of an Angel of Light.
I thought, in my blindness and darkness,
    That he was the Infinite God,
Who had come in the might of his vengeance
    To smite with his merciless rod.

So I cursed Him — and cursed Him — *and cursed*
    Him!
    That He, in his greatness and power,
Had summoned my soul into being,
    And made me to suffer one hour.
I cursed Him for all of my sorrow,
    For all of my weakness and sin,

For all of my hatred and evil,
　　For darkness without and within.

My words were all molten and glowing,
　　As if from a furnace they came,
And the breath of my wrath made them hotter,
　　Till they burned with the fierceness of flame.
Then a light that was in me grew brighter,
　　Like sunshine poured into the heart;
I felt all my burdens grow lighter,
　　And the dross from my nature depart.

"My brother," replied the bright Angel,
　　"Let the name of the Highest be blessed!
Lo! he renders thee blessing for cursing!
　　His will and His way are the best.
Thy soul in His sight hath been precious,
　　Since the birth of thy being began;
Thou art judged by the need of thy nature,
　　And not by the standard of man."

Then out of my cursing and madness,
　　And out of the furnace of flame,
My soul, like a jewel of beauty,

Annealed through life's processes came.
The forms of my loved ones were near me,
The night of my sorrow had passed;
God grant you, O mortals, who judged me,
As full an acceptance at last!

THE EAGLE OF FREEDOM.

O, Land of our glory, our boast, and our pride!
Where the brave and the fearless for Freedom have
    died,
How clear is the lustre that beams from thy
    name!
How bright on thy brow are the laurels of fame!
The stars of thy Union still burn in the sky,
And the scream of thine Eagle is heard from on
    high!
His eyrie is built where no foe can invade,
Nor traitors prevail with the brand and the blade!

CHORUS.

The Eagle of Freedom, in danger and night,
Keeps watch o'er our flag from his star-circled
    height.
From mountain and valley, from hill-top and sea,

Three cheers for the Eagle, the Bird of the Free!
    Hurrah! Hurrah!
Hurrah for the Eagle, the Bird of the Free!

Mount up, O thou Eagle! and rend, in thy flight,
The war-cloud that hides our broad banner from
    sight!
Guard, guard it from danger, though war-rent and
    worn,
And see that no star from its azure is torn!
Keep thy breast to the storm, and thine eye on
    the sun,
Till, true to our motto, THE MANY ARE ONE!
Till the red rage of war with its tumult shall cease,
And the dove shall return with the olive of peace.

CHORUS.

The Eagle of Freedom, in danger and night,
Keeps watch o'er our flag from his star-lighted
    height.
From mountain and valley, from hill-side and sea,
Three cheers for the Eagle, the Bird of the Free!
    Hurrah! Hurrah!
Hurrah for the Eagle, the Bird of the Free!

O, sons of the mighty, the true, and the brave!

The souls of your heroes rest not in the grave:

The holy libation to Liberty poured,

Hath streamed, not in vain, from the blood-crim-
soned sword.

Henceforth, with your **Star-Spangled Banner** unfurled,

Your might shall be felt to the ends of the world,

And rising Republics, like nebulæ, gleam,

Wherever the stars of your nation shall beam.

CHORUS.

The Eagle of Freedom, sublime in his flight,

Shall rest on your banner, encircled with light;

And then shall the chorus, in unison be,

Three cheers for the Eagle, the Bird of the Free!

Hurrah! Hurrah!

Hurrah for the Eagle, the Bird of the Free!

MISTRESS GLENARE.

BY " MARIAN."

A virtuous woman is Mistress Glenare —
  Or, at least, so the world in its judgment would
      say ; —
With an orderly walk and a circumspect air,
  She never departs from the popular way.
Every word that she speaks is well measured and
      weighed ;
  Her friends are selected with scrupulous care;
And in all that she does is her prudence displayed,
  For a virtuous woman is Mistress Glenare !

Her youth has departed, and with it has fled
  The impulse which gives to the blood a new
      start,
Which oftentimes turns from the reasoning head,

To trust to the wisdom of God in the heart.
Thus the robes of her purity never are stained,
  And her feet are withheld from the pitfall and
    snare ;
Where nothing is ventured, there nothing is gained:
  O, a virtuous woman is Mistress Glenare!

She makes no distinction of sinners from sin ;
  Her words are like arrows, her tongue is a rod ;
She sees no excuse for the evil within,
  But condemns with the zeal of a partialist God!
On a background of darkness, of sorrow and shame,
  Her own reputation looks stainless and fair ;
So she builds up her fame, through her neighbors'
    bad name :
  O, a virtuous woman is Mistress Glenare!

She peeps and she listens, she watches and waits,
  Nor Satan himself is more active than she
To expose in poor sinners the faults and bad traits,
  Which she fears that the Lord might not hap-
    pen to see.
When the Father of Spirits looks down from above
  ' On the good and the evil, the frail and the fair,

How must he regard, with *particular* love,
  This virtuous woman — good Mistress Glenare!

O, Mistress Glenare! in the drama of life
  You are acting a *very respectable* part;
You have known just enough of its envious strife
  To deceive both the world and your own fool-
    ish heart.
But say, in some moment of clear common sense,
  Did you never in truth and sincerity dare
To ask the plain question, aside from pretence,
  How you looked to the angels, dear Mistress
    Glenare?

The glory of God has enlightened their eyes:
  No longer, through darkness, they see but in part.
And the robes of your righteousness do not suffice
  To cover the lack of true love in the heart.
You look shabby, and filthy, and ragged, and
    mean —
  E'en with those you condemn, you but poorly
    compare!
Go! wash you in Charity till you are clean;
  You will change for the better, dear Mistress
    Glenare.

Your thoughts have been run in the popular mould.
　Like wax that is plastic and easily melts;
Till now, like a nondescript, lo, and behold!
　You are neither yourself, nor yet any one else.
Of tender compassion, forgiveness, and love,
　Your nature has not a *respectable* share;
You are three parts of serpent, and one of the
　　　dove —
　Very badly proportioned, dear Mistress Glenare.

Your noblest and purest affections have died,
　Like summer-dried roses, your spirit within;
Your heart has grown arid, and scarce is supplied
　With sufficient vitality even to sin.
But would you be true to your virtuous name,
　There is *one* we commend to your tenderest care;
To deal with her wisely will add to your fame:
　That poor sinful woman is — Mistress Glenare.

LITTLE JOHNNY.

[A poem delivered by Miss Lizzie Doten at the close of a lecture in Springfield, May 10, and addressed to the parents of Little Johnny — Mr. and Mrs. Thomas A. Denison, of Chicopee, Mass.]

SING not, O blessed angels!
   To those who truly mourn,
But come with gifts of healing,
   For heart-strings freshly torn.
Ah! human hearts are tender,
   And wounds of love are deep :
Sing not, O blessed angels!
   But "weep with those who weep."

Come not, O spirit-teachers!
   With wisdom from above,
But come with soft, low whispers
   Of sympathy and love.
Truths seem uncertain shadows

Beneath the clouds of care ;
Come, then, in friendly silence,
  And strengthen them to bear.

What will ye bring, O angels,
  To soothe the troubled breast ?
" We will bring the cherished loved one
  From the mansions of the blest.
Like a wandering dove returning,
  He shall nestle in each heart ;
They will feel his blessèd presence,
  And their sorrow shall depart.

" We will lead them from their darkness
  Out to the shining light,
And scenes of heavenly beauty
  Shall greet their longing sight.
There shall they see their loved one,
  Free from his earthly pain ;
Their souls shall cease from sorrow,
  And shall ask him not again.

" O, we only opened gently
  His little prison door ;

He stepped into the sunshine,
  And then returned no more.
He dwells not now in weakness,
  In the spirit's narrow cell,
But yet remains forever
  To those who loved him well."

What will ye bring, O teachers!
  To those who suffer loss?
"We will bring them faith, and patience,
  And strength to bear their cross, —
To bear it bravely, calmly,
  Although the way seem long,
Till hearts that bled with anguish
  Shall burst into a song.

"They shall walk in Faith's clear sunshine,
  With souls renewed in youth,
And the little child shall lead them
  To a knowledge of the truth.
Tell them the loving angels
  Watch o'er their darling boy —
They are sharers of their sorrow,
  And helpers of their joy."

" BIRDIE'S " SPIRIT-SONG.

[At the conclusion of a lecture in Boston, the following poem was addressed to the chairman (Mr. L. B. Wilson). It purported to come from Anna Cora, Mr. Wilson's only child, who passed to the spirit-world at the age of 12 years and 7 months. She was always called by the pet name " Birdie."]

WITH rosebuds in my hand,
Fresh from the Summer-land,
Father, I come and stand
    Close by your side.
You cannot see me here,
Or feel my presence near,
And yet your " Birdie " dear
    Never has died.

O, no! for angels bright,
Out of the blessèd light,
Shone on my wondering sight,
    Singing, " We come!

7

Lamb for the fold above —
Tender, young, nestling dove —
Safe in our arms of love,
    Haste to thy home."

Mother! I could not stay;
In a sweet dream I lay,
Wafted to Heaven away,
    Far from the night;
Then, with a glad surprise,
Did I unclose my eyes,
Under those cloudless skies,
    Smiling with light!

O! were you with me there,
Free from your earthly care,
All of my joy to share,
    I were more blest.
But it is best to stay
Here in the earthly way,
Till the good angels say,
    "Come to your rest! '

Check, then, the falling tear;
Think of me still as near.

Father and mother dear,
  Soon on that shore,
Where all the loved ones meet,
Resting your pilgrim feet,
Shall you with blessings greet
  " Birdie " once more.

MY SPIRIT-HOME.

"We find the following beautiful stanzas in the Evening Courier, published in Portland, Me. They were composed in spirit-life by Miss A. W. Sprague, and spoken under spirit-influence by Miss Lizzie Doten, at the close of her lecture in that city, on Sunday evening, March 22d. The lines are evidently from the spirit of Miss Sprague, who passed to the spirit-world last summer, from her home in Vermont, as there are allusions in it to incidents which took place during her illness, in Oswego, N. Y., about a year since. Allusion is also made to a poem written by her and published in the *Banner*, and also to another poem of hers, 'I wait, I wait at the golden gate.' " — *Banner of Light.*

I come, I come from my spirit-home,
　　Like a bird in the early spring,
To the loved ones here, whom my heart holds dear,
　　A message of love to bring.
O, the heavens are wide, but they cannot divide
　　The spirits whom love makes free!
The green old earth, and the land of my birth,
　　With its homes, are still dear to me.

The phantoms of pain in my burning brain
    Have fled from the Heaven's clear light;
I lie no more on the lake's lone shore,
    In the fever dreams of night.
O, it was not late when I fled from fate,
    And that which the world calls sin;
No longer "I wait at the golden gate,"
    For the angels have let me in.

O, not too soon, though at life's high noon,
    Was the close of my earthly day;
As the roses fade, ere the evening shade,
    I passed from the earth away.
And I knew not the blight of the bitter night,
    Which withers the autumn flowers,
Or the lengthening years, with their weight of tears,
    That burden the spirit's powers.

In the forest wide, by the lake's green side,
    The angels had whispered low;
From "over the sea" they had called to me,
    And I knew that I soon must go:
But I felt no fear when I knew they were near,
    Nor shrank from the narrow way,

For I caught faint gleams of the crystal streams.
    And the light of the heavenly day.

O! the angels bright, with their robes of light,
    The clasp of each gentle hand,
And the eyes that smiled on earth's weary child.
    As I entered the better land!
But words are weak when the soul would speak
    Of the angel-home above;
Faint visions alone are to man made known,
    Of that dwelling of light and love.

My home is there, in that world so fair,
    But the space is not deep or wide
Which lies between this earthly scene
    And the home on the other side.
The thought of love, like a carrier dove,
    Shall the heart's fond message bear,
And the angel bands, with their willing hands,
    Shall answer each earnest prayer.

Fare ye well! farewell! My spirit can dwell
    In the earthly form no more;
But whither I go, and the *way*, ye shall know,

To your home on the other shore.
Soon "over the sea" ye shall walk with me,
On the hills by the angels trod,
In the garments white, of the sons of light,
In the freedom and peace of God.

I STILL LIVE.

[Given under the inspiration of Miss A. W. Sprague, at the conclusion of a lecture in Philadelphia, October 25, 1863.]

O THOU, whose love is changeless,
    Both now and evermore;
Source of all conscious being.
    Thy goodness I adore.
Lord, I would ever praise Thee,
    For all Thy love can give;
But most of all, O Father!
    I thank Thee that I live.

I live! O ye who loved me!
    Your faith was not in vain;
Back through the shadowy valley
    I come to you again.
Safe in the love that guides me,
    With fearless feet I tread —

My home is with the angels —
  O, say not I am dead!

Not dead! O, no, but lifted
  Above all earthly strife;
Now first I know the meaning,
  And feel the power of life —
The power to rise uncumbered
  By woe, or want, or care;
To breathe ·fresh inspiration
  From pure, celestial air; —

To feel that all the tempests
  Of human life have passed,
And that my ark, in safety rests
  On the mount at last;
To send my soul's great longings,
  Like Noah's dove, abroad,
And find them swift returning,
  With signs of peace from God; —

To soar in fearless freedom
  Through broad, blue, boundless skies
And catch the radiant gleaming

Of love-lit, angel eyes;
To feel the Father's presence
Around me, near or far,
And see His radiant glory
Stretch onward, star by star; —

To feel those grand upliftings
That know not space nor time;
To hear all discords ending
In harmony sublime;
To know that sin and error
Are dimly understood,
And that which man calls Evil
Is undeveloped Good; —

To stand in spell-bound rapture
On some celestial height,
And see God's glorious sunshine
Dispel the shades of night;
To feel that all creation
With love and joy is rife; —
This, O my earthly loved ones,
This is Eternal Life!

There, eyes that closed in darkness
   Shall open to the morn;
And those whom death had stricken,
   Shall find themselves new-born;
The lame shall leap with gladness,
   The blind rejoice to see;
The slave shall know no master.
   And the prisoner shall be free.

There, the worn and heavy-laden
   Their burdens shall lay down;
There, crosses, borne in meekness,
   At length shall win the crown;
And lonely hearts that famished
   For sympathy and love,
Shall find a free affection
   In the angel-home above.

O, children of our Father!
   Weep not for those who pass,
Like rose-leaves gently scattered,
   Like dew-drops from the grass.
Ay, look not down in sadness,
   But fix your gaze on high;

They only dropped their mantles —
　　Their souls can never die.

They live! and still unbroken
　　Is that magnetic chain,
Which, in your tearful blindness,
　　You thought was rent in twain.
That chain of love was fashioned
　　By more than human art,
And every link is welded
　　So firm it cannot part.

They live! but O, not idly,
　　To fold their hands to rest,
For they who love God truly,
　　Are they who serve him best.
Love lightens all their labor,
　　And makes all duty sweet;
Their hands are never weary,
　　Nor way-worn are their feet.

Thus by that world of beauty,
　　And by that life of love,
And by the holy angels

Who listen now above,
I pledge my soul's endeavor,
  To do whate'er I can
To bless my sister woman,
  And aid my brother man.

O Thou, whose love is changeless,
  Both now and evermore,
Source of all conscious being!
  Thy goodness I adore.
Lord, I would ever praise Thee
  For all Thy love can give;
But most of all, O Father,
  I thank Thee that I live.

8

[The two following poems were given under an influence purporting to be that of Shakspeare.]

LIFE.

"To be, or not to be," is not "the question;"
There is no choice of Life. Ay, mark it well!—
For Death is but another name for Change.
The weary shuffle off their mortal coil,
And think to slumber in eternal night.
But, lo! the man, though dead, is living still;
Unclothed, is clothed upon, and his Mortality
Is swallowed up of Life.

"He babbles o' green fields, then falls asleep,"
And straight awakes amid eternal verdure.
Fairer than "dreams of a Midsummer's Night,"
The fields Elysian stretch before him.
No "Tempest" rends the ever peaceful bowers
Of asphodel, and fadeless amaranth;

No hot sirocco blows with poisonous breath;
No midnight frights him with its goblins grim,
Presaging sudden death. No Macbeth there,
Mad with ambition, plotteth damning deeds;
No Hamlet, haunted by his father's ghost,
Stalks wildly forth intent on vengeance dire.
The curse of Cain on earth is consummate,
And knows no resurrection. Spirits learn
That spirit is immortal, and no poisoned cup,
Or dagger's thrust, or sting of deadly asp,
Can rob it of its Godlike attribute.
This mortal garb may be as full of wounds
And bloody rents as royal Caesar's mantle;
Yet that which made it man or Caesar liveth still.

Man learns, in this Valhalla of his soul,
To love, nor ever finds "Love's Labor Lost."
No two-faced Falstaff proffers double suit;
No Desdemona mourns Iago's art;
And every Romeo finds his Juliet.
The stroke of Death is but a kindly frost,
Which cracks the shell, and leaves the kernel room
To germinate. What most consummate fools
This fear of death doth make us! Reason plays

The craven unto sense, and in her fear
Chooses the slow and slavish death of life,
Rather than freedom in the life of death.
" Thus *Ignorance* makes cowards of us all,"
And blinds us to our being's best estate.
Madly we cling to life through nameless ills,
Pinched by necessity, and scourged by fate,
Fainting in heat and freezing in the cold,
While war, and pestilence, and sore distress,
Fever and famine, fire and flood, combine
To drive the spirit from its wreck of clay.

O, poor Humanity! How full of blots,
And stains, and pains, and miseries thou art!
Here let me be thine Antony, and plead
Thy cause against the slayers of thy peace.
Though wounded, yet thou art not dead, thou child
Of Immortality — thou heir of God!
He who would slay thee, be he brute or Brutus,
Plunges the dagger in his own vile heart.
And yet thy wounds are piteous. I could weep
That aught so fair from the Creator's hand
Should be so marred and mangled, like a lamb
Torn by the ravening wolves. Here, let me take

Thy mantle, pierced with gaping, ghastly wounds,
From daggers clutched by ingrate hands. O Truth!
How many, in thy sacred name, have slain
Humanity, thinking they did God service!
Rome, and not Cæsar — Doctrines, and not Men.

I cannot count the wounds which lust for power,
And wealth, and place, and precedence have made.
But, O! the keenest, deepest, deadliest stabs
Of all, were made by false Philosophy
And false Theology combined —
Philosophy, that knew not what it did;
Theology, that did not what it knew.
See here! This rent made by the fear of God,
That gracious God, whose "mercy seasons justice,"
Who feeds the raven, clothes the lilies, heeds
The sparrow when it falls, and sends his rain
Alike upon the evil and the good.
And yet they were all "honorable men"
Who taught this doctrine — "*honorable men!*"
Whose failing was a lack of common sense.

And, lo! here is another — Fear of Truth —
Blind Superstition made this horrid rent,

And Bigotry quick followed up the thrust.
O, 'tis an eye weeping great tears of blood!
An eagle eye, that dared to love the light
Which Bigotry and Superstition feared,
Lest it should make their deeds of evil plain.
Thus is it, he who dares to see a Truth
Not recognized in creeds, must die the death.
But noon-day never stayed for bats and owls,
And Truth's clear light shall yet arise and shine.

 See here: another wound—The fear of Death—
That blessèd consummation of this life,
Which soothes all pain, makes good all loss, revives
The weak, gives rest and peace, makes free the
   slave,
Levels all past distinctions, and doth place
The beggar on a footing with the king.
O, poor Humanity! those who conspired
To slay thee, through exceeding love for God,
And for the glory of His mighty name,
Smote at the very centre of thy peace,
And damning doubts, like daggers' thrusts, attest
How zealously they aimed each cruel blow.

And yet, this rent and bloody mantle is not thee.
Slain, but not dead — thy spirit shall arise
And face thy startled enemies again,
As royal Cæsar's ghost appeared to Brutus,
In Sardis' and Philippi's tented plains.
Thou royal heir to kingdoms yet unknown!
A mightier than Cæsar is thy Friend.
He stays the hand of Cassius, Brutus, all
Who aim their weapons at thy life, and dulls
Their daggers' points against thy deathless soul.
From every gaping wound of fear or doubt,
Murder or malice, sorrow or despair,
Thy spirit leaps as from a prison door.
It laughs at death and daggers, as it flies
To hold companionship with spirits blest;
And having thus informed itself of life,
The question then, — "To be, or not to be?" —
Is swallowed up in Immortality.

LOVE.

[Shakspeare.]

O World! somewhat I have to say to thee.
O sin-sick, heart-sick, soul-sick, love-sick World!
So ailing art thou, both in part and particle,
That solid truth thy stomach ill digests.
Yet, since thou art my mother, I will love thee,
And heedless of thy frowns, "will speak right on."

That which belongs to all men is least prized;
The thing most common is least understood.
That which is deep and silent is divine;
And there is nought on earth so craved, so common,
So misunderstood, or so divine, as Love.
When meted in proportion to man's need,
"Measure for measure" it doth purify,
Exalt, and make him equal with the gods.

He feeds upon ambrosia, and his drink
Is nectar; high Olympus cannot yield
Delights more grateful to his soul and sense.
Parnassus fails his rapture to express,
And Helicon hath less of inspiration.
But, prithee, should he chance to drink too deep
Of the exhilarating draught, — should plunge
Him head and ears into this 'wildering flood, —
Mark, then, what marvellous diversions
From the centre of his gravity ensue.
Judgment is scouted — sober common sense
Yields to imagination's airy flights:
Upon a swift-winged hippogriff he mounts,
To seek the fair Arcadia of his dreams.
He builds him castles — basks in moonshine —
      feeds
Among the lilies — pours his passion forth
In amorous canticles and burning sighs —
Makes him a bed of roses, and lies down
To revel in his rainbow-colored dreams —
Until some turn, some ill-begotten chance,
Most unexpectedly invades his peace,
And castles, moonshine, roses, rainbows fly,
And leave him to the stern realities of life.

Alas, poor Human Nature! Even fools
Must learn through sad experience to grow wise.

Love is the highest attribute of Deity;
And he who loves divinely is most blest.
It purgeth passion from the soul and sense,
And makes the man a unit in himself;
Head, eyes, hands, heart, all work in unison,
And beasts, and savages, and rudest hinds,
All feel alike its exercise of power.

Ambition cannot walk with it; for he
Who learns to live and love aright, loves all,
And finds preferment in the general weal.
Though, Proteus like, it takes a thousand forms,
It doth o'ercome all evil with its good,
Casteth out devils — sensuality, and sin,
And green-eyed jealousy, and hate; and like
Chrysostom, golden-mouthed, it doth attune
The words of common speech to sweet accord,
And gives significance to simplest things.

It buddeth out in tender infancy,
Like fresh-blown violets in the early spring,

And giveth form and fashion to all life.
For, by its character, it doth decide
What elements and essences the soul
Shall draw from contact with material things.
As roses draw their blushes, lilies whiteness,
Violets their azure, from the same dull earth,
So Love extracts the sweetnesses of Life,
And doth so mingle all within her crucible,
That she creates the difference between
Immortal souls.   The fiery heart of youth,
Full of high aims and generous purposes of good,
Swells like the ocean-waves beneath the moon,
And brooketh no restraint, until it finds
Its living counterpart, and mergeth all
It hath of truth, and manliness, and might,
Into a second and a dearer self.

　　So goes the world! and strong necessity
Creates the law of action, whose results
Join issue with the love of God himself.
O jealous, wanton, ill-conceited World!
How little dost thou understand the deep
Significance and potency of Love!
Thou hast defiled thyself with gross perversions,

Till purity of love is but a jest,
Or reckoned with the fantasies of fools.

O, I would take thee, dear Humanity,
And set thee face to face with perfect Love.
She is thy mother.   Love and Wisdom met
United by Eternal Power.   The worlds
Sprang forth from chaos; and the love which
        brought
Them into being doth sustain them still.
The monad and the angel rest alike
Within its all-embracing arms; and life,
And death, with all that makes our mortal state,
Are cradled at the footstool of this power.
Then, sweet Humanity, thou favored child
Of God, look up!   An everlasting chain
Doth bind thee to the mighty heart of all.
Love's labor never can be lost.   He who
Created, shall, through Love, perfect and save;
And that which hath such poor expression here,
Shall find fruition in a brighter sphere.

FOR A' THAT.

[The following poem was given under the inspiration of Robert Burns.]

Is there a luckless wight on earth,
 Oppressed wi' care and a' that,
Who holds his life as little worth,
 His home is Heaven for a' that —
  For a' that, and a' that.
 There's muckle joy for a' that;
He's seen the warst o' hell below,
 His home is Heaven for a' that.

The weary slave that drags his chain,
 In toil and grief, and a' that,
Shall find relief from a' his pain,
 And rest in Heaven from a' that.
  From a' that and a' that.
 There's freedom there from a' that,

For Justice throws into the scale
　A recompense for a' that.

Puir souls, in right not unco strong,
　Through love and want and a' that,
There sure is power to right their wrong,
　And save their souls, for a' that —
　　For a' that, and a' that.
　The Lord is guid for a' that;
The de'il himsel' can turn and mend,
　And come to Heaven for a' that.

On Scotia's hills the gowans spring,
　The heather blooms, and a' that;
The mavis and the merlé sing,
　But Heaven's my home for a' that —
　　For a' that, and a' that.
　I wadna' change for a' that.
He who once finds the Heaven aboon
　Will not come back for a' that.

WORDS O' CHEER.

[Given under the inspiration of Robert Burns.]

GUID FRIENDS:

    Although not present to your sight,

I gie ye greeting here to-night;

Not claiming to be perfect quite,

    Frae taint o' passion,

Yet will I hauld my speech aright,

    In guid Scotch fashion.

O, could some cantic * word o' mine,

But make your careworn faces shine,

Or cause the hearts in grief that pine,

    To throb with pleasure,

Then wad my cup to auld lang syne,

    Fill to its measure.

* Cheerful.

The gracious powers above us, know
How sair a weight of want and woe
Must be the lot of those who go
  Through Earth to Heaven;
But aye, the life aboon will show
  Wherefore 'twas given.

And that guid God who loves us a',
Who sees the chittering * sparrow fa',
Will never turn his face awa',
  Though you should stray;
But all his wandering sheep will ca'
  Back to the way.

So muckle † are the cares o' men,
That Truth at times is hard to ken,
And Error, to her grousome ‡ den,
  So dark and eerie,
Wiles those who have na heart to men'; §
  Puir wanderers weary.

Alack! how mony a luckless wight
Has gane agley ‖ in Error's night,

---

* Trembling. † Great. ‡ Gloomy. § Amend. ‖ Astray.

Not that he had less love for right
    Than countless ithers;
But that he lacked the keener sight
    Of his guid brithers.

Lo! Calvin, Knox, and Luther, cry
"I have the Truth" — "and I" — "and I." —
"Puir sinners! if ye gang agley,
    The de'il will hae ye,
And then the Lord will stand abeigh,
    And will na save ye."

But hoolie* hoolie! Na sae fast;
When Gabriél shall blaw his blast,
And Heaven and Earth awa' have passed,
    These lang syne saints,
Shall find baith de'il and hell at last,
    Mere pious feints.

The upright, honest-hearted man,
Who strives to do the best he can,
Need never fear the Church's ban,
    Or hell's damnation;

* Stop.

For God will need na special plan
 For his salvation.

The one who knows our deepest needs,
Recks little how man counts his beads,
For Righteousness is not in creeds,
 Or solemn faces;
But rather lies in kindly deeds,
 And Christian graces,

Then never fear; wi' purpose leal, *
A head to think, a heart to feel
For human woe and human weal,
 Na preachin' loun †
Your sacred birthright e'er can steal
 To Heaven aboon.

Tak' ‡ tent o' truth, and heed this well:
The man who sins makes his ain hell;
There's na waurse de'il than himsel';
 But God is strongest:
And when puir human hearts rebel,
 He haulds out longest.

---

 * True.   † Follow.   ‡ Pay attention.

With loving kindness will he wait,
Till all the prodigals o' fate
Return unto their fair estate,
    And blessings mony;
Nor will he shut the gowden gate
    Of Heaven on ony.

.

RESURREXI.

"A REMARKABLE POEM.—The following striking poem was recited by Miss Lizzie Doten, a Spiritual trance-speaker, at the close of a recent lecture in Boston. She professed to give it impromptu, as far as she was concerned, and to speak under the direct influence of Edgar A. Poe. Whatever may be the truth about its production, the poem is, in several respects, a remarkable one. Miss Doten is, apparently, incapable of originating such a poem. If it was written for her by some one else, and merely committed to memory and recited by her, the poem is, nevertheless, wonderful as a reproduction of the singular music and alliteration of Poe's style, and as manifesting the same intensity of feeling. Whoever wrote the poem must have been exceedingly familiar with Poe, and deeply in sympathy with his spirit. But if Miss Doten is honest, and the poem originated as she said it did, it is unquestionably the most astonishing thing that Spiritualism has produced. It does not follow, necessarily, in that case, that Poe himself made the poem,—although we are asked to believe a great many spiritual things on less cogent evidence,—but it is, in any view of it that may be taken, a very singular and mysterious production. There is, in the second verse, an allusion to a previous poem that purported to come from the spirit of Poe, which was published several years since, and attracted much attention, but the following poem is of a higher order, and much more like Poe than the other."— *Springfield Republican.*

FROM the throne of Life Eternal,
From the home of love supernal,

Where the angel feet make music over all the starry
    floor —
Mortals, I have come to meet you,
Come with words of peace to greet you,
And to tell you of the glory that is mine forever-
    more.

Once before I found a mortal
Waiting at the heavenly portal —
Waiting but to catch some echo from that ever-
    opening door;
Then I seized his quickened being,
And through all his inward seeing,
Caused my burning inspiration in a fiery flood to
    pour!

Now I come more meekly human,
And the weak lips of a woman
Touch with fire from off the altar, not with burn-
    ings as of yore;
But in holy love descending,
With her chastened being blending,
I would fill your souls with music from the bright
    celestial shore.

As one heart yearns for another,

As a child turns to its mother,

From the golden gates of glory turn I to the earth

once more,

Where I drained the cup of sadness,

Where my soul was stung to madness,

And life's bitter, burning billows swept my burdened

being o'er.

Here the harpies and the ravens, —

Human vampyres, sordid cravens, —

Preyed upon my soul and substance till I writhed in

anguish sore;

Life and I then seemed mismated,

For I felt accursed and fated,

Like a restless, wrathful spirit, wandering on the

Stygian shore.

Tortured by a nameless yearning,

Like a frost-fire, freezing, burning,

Did the purple, pulsing life-tide through its fevered

channels pour,

Till the golden bowl — Life's token —

Into shining shards was broken,
And my chained and chafing spirit leaped from out
its prison door.

But while living, striving, dying,
Never did my soul cease crying,
" Ye who guide the Fates and Furies, give, O give
me, I implore,
From the myriad hosts of nations,
From the countless constellations,
One pure spirit that can love me — one that I, too,
can adore !"

Through this fervent aspiration
Found my fainting soul salvation,
For from out its blackened fire-crypts did my quick-
ened spirit soar;
And my beautiful ideal —
Not too saintly to be real —
Burst more brightly on my vision than the loved and
lost Lenore.

'Mid the surging seas she found me.
With the billows breaking round me,

And my saddened, sinking spirit in her arms of love
    upbore ;
    Like a lone one, weak and weary,
    Wandering in the midnight dreary,
On her sinless, saintly bosom, brought me to the
    heavenly shore.

    Like the breath of blossoms blending,
    Like the prayers of saints ascending,
Like the rainbow's seven-hued glory, blend *our* souls
    forevermore ;
    Earthly love and lust enslaved me,
    But divinest love hath saved me,
And I know now, first and only, how to love and to
    adore.

    O, my mortal friends and brothers!
    We are each and all another's,
And the soul that gives most freely from its treasure
    hath the more ;
    Would you lose your life, you find it,
    And in giving love, you bind it
Like an amulet of safety, to your heart forevermore.

THE PROPHECY OF VALA.

[Given under the inspiration of Edgar A. Poe.]

The Prophecy of Vala is founded on the Scandinavian mythology. Odin, the great All Father, is the sovereign power of the universe; Thor, a lesser god, of whom it is said, "his mighty hammer smote thunder out of every thing." Baldur was a son of Odin and Frigga. He was slain by Hörder, his blind brother, who was persuaded to the act by Loke, an evil spirit, corresponding to the Hebrew or Christian devil. The Valkyrien were the genii of the battle-field. The three Nornen were the Fates who watered the tree Yggdrasill, at whose roots it is said that a dragon was constantly gnawing. The Heimskringla was the circle of the universe. Vala was a seeress, or prophetess, who was summoned from the dead by Odin, to tell of the fate of Baldur; but on her appearance refused to do so, and to the astonishment of all, prophesied the death of all the sons of Odin at the day of Regnaroc, which corresponds to the day of judgment, with the exception that it was also the day of reconstruction, or renewal of the world. The Prophecy of Vala, as given in the old Icelandic Edda, has been used with perfect freedom, to present the idea that Good, though apparently overcome of Evil, should ultimately triumph. — *Explanation by Poe.*

I HAVE walked with the Fates and the Furies 'mid
    the wrecks of the mighty Past,
I have stood in the giant shadows which the ages
    have backward cast,

And I've heard the voices of prophets come down
    in a lengthening chain,
Translating the Truth Eternal, and making its
    meaning plain;
Backward still, ever backward, 'mid wreck and
    ruin I trod,
Seeking Life's secret sources, and the primal truths
    of God.

"Tell me," I cried, "O Prophet, thou shade of
    the mighty Past,
What of the Truth in the future? Is its horoscope
    yet cast?
Thou didst give it its birth and being, thou didst
    cradle it in thy breast —
Show me its shining orbit, and the place of its
    final rest!"

A sound like the restless earthquake! a crash like
    the "crack of doom"!
And a fiery fulmination streamed in through the
    frightened gloom.
I stood in the halls of Odin, and the great All
    Father shone

Like the centre and sun of Being, 'mid the glories
    of his throne;
And Thor, with his mighty hammer, upraised in
    his giant hand,
Stood ready to wake the thunder at his sovereign
    Lord's command.

"Ho, Thor!" said the mighty Odin, "our omens
    are all of ill,
For the dragon gnaweth sharply at the roots of
    Yggdrasill;
I hear the wild Valkyrien, as they shriek on the
    battle-plain,
And the moans of the faithful Nornen, as they
    weep over Baldur slain.
A woe to the serpent Loké, and to Hörder's
    reckless ruth,
For Goodness is slain of Evil, and Falsehood hath
    conquered Truth!
Now call thou on mystic Vala, as she sleeps in
    the grave of Time,
Where the hoary age hath written her name in a
    frosty rime;

She can tell when the sun will darken, when the
    stars shall cease to burn,
When the sleeping dead shall waken, and when
    Baldur shall return."

A sound like the rushing tempest, and the won-
    drous hammer fell,
And the great Heimskringla shuddered, and swayed
    like a mighty bell.
There were mingled murmurs and discords, like
    the wailing of troubled souls;
Like the gnomes at their fiery forges — like the
    howlings of restless ghouls.
Then out of the fiery covert of the tempest and
    the storm,
Like a vision of troubled slumber, came a woman's
    stately form.
There fell a hush as at midnight, when the sheeted
    dead awake,
And even the silence shuddered, as her words of
    power she spake:

"Mighty Odin, I am Vala,
    I have heard your thunder-call,

I have heard the woful wailing
    Sounding forth from Wingolf's hall;
And I know that beauteous Baldur,
    Loved of all the gods, is slain —
That the evil Loké triumphs,
    And on Hörder rests the stain.
But my words shall fail to tell you
    Aught concerning him you mourn,
For the leaves that bear the record
    From the Tree of Life are torn;
And while Hecla's fires shall glow,
Or the bubbling Geysers flow,
Of his fate no one shall know —
Understand you this, or no?

"I will sing a solemn Saga,
    I will chant a Runic rhyme,
Weave a wild, prophetic Edda,
    From the scattered threads of time:
Know, O Odin, — mighty Odin, —
    That thy sons shall all be slain,
Where the wild Valkyrien gather,
    On the bloody battle plain;
And thy throne itself shall tremble

10 *

With the stern, resistless shock,
Which shall rend the world asunder
    At the day of Ragnaroe.
Other stars the night shall know,
From the rock shall waters flow,
And from ruin beauty grow.
Understand you this, or no?

"Vainly shall the faithful Nornen
    Water drooping Yggdrasill,
For the wrathful, restless dragon
    At its roots is gnawing still.
Loké's evil arts shall triumph,
    Hörder's eyes be dark with night,
Till the day of re-creation
    Brings the buried Truth to light:
Then a greater god than Odin,
    Over all the worlds shall reign,
And my Saga's mystic meaning,
    As the sunlight shall be plain.
Out of evil good shall grow —
Doubt me not, for time shall show.
Understand you this, or no?
Fare you well! I go — I go!"

There came a voice as of thunder, with a gleam of
    lurid light,
And the mystic Vala vanished like a meteor of
    the night;
Then I saw that the truth of the present is but
    the truth of the past,
But each phase is greater, and grander, and
    mightier than the last —
That the past is ever prophetic of that which is
    yet to be,
And that God reveals his glory by slow and dis-
    tinct degree;
Yet still are the nations weeping o'er the graves
    of the Truth and Right:
Lo! I summon another Vala — let her prophesy
    to-night.
With the amaranth, and the myrtle, and the aspho-
    del on her brow,
Still wet with the dew of the kingdom, doth she
    stand before you now:

    "Not with sound of many thunders,
    Not with miracles and wonders,
Would I herald forth my coming from the peace-
    ful spirit-shore;

But in God's own love descending,
With your aspirations blending,
I would teach you of the future, that you watch
    and weep no more.

"God is God from the creation;
    Truth, alone, is man's salvation:
But the God that now you worship soon shall be
    your God no more;
For the soul, in its unfolding,
    Evermore its thought remoulding,
Learns more truly, in its progress, 'how to love
    and to adore!'

"Evil is of Good, twin brother,
    Born of God, and of none other:
And though Truth seems slain of Error, through
    the ills that men deplore,
Yet, still nearer to perfection,
    She shall know a resurrection,
Passing on from ceaseless glory, unto glory ever-
    more.

"From the truths of former ages,
    From the world's close-lettered pages,

Man shall learn to meet more bravely all the life
      that lies before;
    For the day of retribution
    Is the final restitution
Of the good, the true, the holy, which shall live
      forevermore!
    'Understand you this, or no?
    Fare you well! I go — I go!'"

THE KINGDOM.

[Given under the inspiration of Poe.]

" And I saw no temple therein." — *Rev.* 21 : 22.

'Twas the ominous month of October —
　How the memories rise in my soul!
　How they swell like a sea in my soul! —
When a spirit, sad, silent, and sober,
　Whose glance was a word of control,
Drew me down to the dark Lake Avernus,
　In the desolate Kingdom of Death —
To the mist-covered Lake of Avernus,
　In the ghoul-haunted Kingdom of Death.

And there, as I shivered and waited,
　I talked with the Souls of the Dead —
　With those whom the living call dead;
The lawless, the lone, and the hated,

Who broke from their bondage and fled —
From madness and misery fled.
Each word was a burning eruption
That leapt from a crater of flame —
A red, lava-tide of corruption,
That out of life's sediment came, ·
From the scoriac natures God gave them,
Compounded of glory and shame.

"Aboard!" cries our pilot and leader;
Then wildly we rush to embark,
We recklessly rush to embark;
And forth in our ghostly Ellida*
We swept in the silence and dark —
O God! on that black Lake Avernus,
Where vampyres drink even the breath,
On that terrible Lake of Avernus,
Leading down to the whirlpool of Death!

It was there the Eumenides† found us,
In sight of no shelter or shore —
No beacon or light from the shore.

* The dragon ship of the Norse mythology.
† The Fates and Furies.

They lashed up the white waves around us,
  We sank in the waters' wild roar;
But not to the regions infernal,
  Through billows of sulphurous flame,
But unto the City Eternal,
  The Home of the Blesséd, we came.

To the gate of the Beautiful City,
  All fainting and weary we pressed,
  Impatient and hopeful we pressed.
"O, Heart of the Holy, take pity,
  And welcome us home to our rest!
Pursued by the Fates and the Furies,
  In darkness and danger we fled —
From the pitiless Fates and the Furies,
  Through the desolate realms of the Dead."

"*Jure Divino*, I here claim admission!"
  Exclaimed a proud prelate, who rushed to the
    gate;
"*Ave Sanctissima*, hear my petition
  Holy Saint Peter; O, why should I wait?
O, *fons pietatis*, O, glorious flood,
My soul is washed clean in the Lamb's precious
    blood."

Like the song of a bird that yet lingers,
    When the wide-wandering warbler has flown;
    Like the wind-harp by Eolus blown,
As if touched by the lightest of fingers,
    The portal wide open was thrown;
And we saw — not the holy Saint Peter,
    Not even an angel of light,
But a vision far dearer and sweeter,
    Not brilliant nor blindingly bright,
    But marvellous unto the sight!

In the midst of the mystical splendor,
    Stood a beautiful, beautiful child —
    A golden-haired, azure-eyed child.
With a look that was touching and tender,
    She stretched out her white hand and smiled.
"Ay, welcome, thrice welcome, poor mortals.
    O, why do ye linger and wait?
Come fearlessly in at these portals —
    No warder keeps watch at the gate!"

"*Gloria Deo! Te Deum laudamus!*"
    Exclaimed the proud prelate, "I'm safe into
        Heaven;

11

Through the blood of the Lamb, and the martyrs
    who claim us,
  My soul has been purchased, my sins are for-
    given!
I tread where the saints and the martyrs have
    trod —
Lead on, thou fair child, to the temple of God!"

  The child stood in silence and wonder,
    Then bowed down her beautiful head,
    And even as fragrance is shed
From the lily the waves have swept under,
    She meekly and tenderly said —
    So simply and truthfully said:
"In vain do ye seek to behold Him;
    He dwells in no temple apart;
The height of the Heavens cannot hold him,
    And yet he is here in my heart —
    He is here, and he will not depart."

  Then out from the mystical splendor,
    The swift-changing, crystalline light,
    The rainbow-hued, scintillant light,
Gleamed faces more touching and tender

Than ever had greeted our sight —
Our sin-blinded, death-darkened sight;
And they sang: " Welcome home to the Kingdom,
Ye earth-born and serpent-beguiled;
The Lord is the light of this Kingdom,
And His temple the heart of a child —
Of a trustful and teachable child,
Ye are born to the life of the Kingdom —
Receive, and believe, as a child."

THE CRADLE OR COFFIN.

[Given under the inspiration of Poe.]

THE Cradle or Coffin, the robe or the shroud,
Of which shall a mortal most truly be proud?
The cradle rocks light as a boat on the billow,
The child lies asleep on his soft, downy pillow,
    And the mother sits near with her love-lighted
        eyes, —
Sits watching her treasure, and dreamily singing,
While the cradle keeps time, like a pendulum
        swinging,
    And notes every moment of bliss as it flies.

Lullaby baby — watch o'er his rest!
The dear little fledgling asleep in his nest.
How blest is that slumber — how calm he reposes,
With his sweet, pouting lips, and his cheeks flushed
    with roses!

O, God of the Innocent, would it might last!
But know, thou fond mother, beyond thy perceiving,
The Parcæ are near him, and steadily weaving
    The meshes of Fate which around him they cast!

Lullaby baby —let him not wake!
Soon shall the bubble of infancy break;
Life, with its terrors and fears, shall surround him,
Evil and Good with strange problems confound
        him,
  And, as the charmed bird to the serpent is drawn,
The demons of hell, from his proudest position,
Shall drag down his soul to the depths of perdi-
        tion,
    Till he bitterly curses the day he was born!

  The Cradle or Coffin, the blanket or pall—
  O, which brings a blessing of peace unto all?
How still is the Coffin! No undulant motion;
Becalmed like a boat on the breast of the ocean.
  And there lies the child, with his half-curtained
    eyes,
While his mother stands near him, her love-watch
    still keeping,

11 *

And kisses his pale lips with wailing and weeping,
　Till her anguish is dumb, or can speak but in
　　sighs.　　　　　．

　He needs not a lullaby now for his rest;
　The fledgling has fluttered, and flown from his
　　nest.
He starts not, he breathes not, he knows no awak-
　ing,
Though sad eyes are weeping and fond hearts are
　breaking.
　O, God of all mercy, how strange are thy ways!
Yet know, thou fond mother, beyond thy per-
　ceiving,
The angels who took him are tenderly weaving
　His vestments of beauty, his garments of praise.

　O, call him not back to earth's weariness now,
　For blossoms unfading encircle his brow;
From glory to glory forever ascending,
His soul with the soul of the Infinite blending,
　Great luminous truths on his being shall dawn.
With no doubts to distract him, or stay his en-
　deavor,

He shall bless in his progress, forever and ever,
  The day that his soul to the Kingdom was born.

The Cradle or Coffin, the robe or the shroud,
Of which shall a mortal most truly be proud?
The Cradle or Coffin, the blanket or pall,
O, which brings a blessing of peace unto all?
The Cradle or Coffin, both places of rest —
Tell us, O mortals, which like ye the best?

THE STREETS OF BALTIMORE.

" EDGAR A. POE. — As the circumstances attendant upon the death
of Poe are not generally known, it may be well to present the facts
in connection with the following poem. Having occasion to pass
through Baltimore a few days before his intended marriage with a
lady of family and fortune in Virginia, Poe met with some of his old
associates, who induced him to drink with them, although, as we are
informed, he had entirely abstained for a year. This aroused the appetite which had so long slumbered within him, and in a short time he
wandered forth into the street in a state of drunken delirium, and was
found next morning literally dying from exposure. He was taken to
a hospital, and on the 7th of October, 1849, at the age of thirty-eight,
he closed his troubled life. The tortures and terrors of that night of
suffering are vividly portrayed in the following poem, composed in
spirit-life, and given by him through the mediumship of Miss Lizzie
Doten, at the conclusion of her lecture in Baltimore, on Sunday evening, January 11, 1863." — *Banner of Light.*

WOMAN weak, and woman mortal,
Through thy spirit's open portal,
   I would read the Runic record
      Of mine earthly being o'er —
I would feel that fire returning,
Which within my soul was burning,

When my star was quenched in darkness,
   Set, to rise on earth no more,
When I sank beneath life's burden
   In the streets of Baltimore!

O, those memories, sore and saddening!
O, that night of anguish maddening!
   When my lone heart suffered shipwreck
    On a demon-haunted shore —
When the fiends grew wild with laughter,
And the silence following after,
   Was more awful and appalling
    Than the cannon s deadly roar —
Than the tramp of mighty armies
   Through the streets of Baltimore!

Like a fiery serpent coiling,
Like a Maelstrom madly boiling,
   Did this Phlegethon of fury
    Sweep my shuddering spirit o'er!
Rushing onward, blindly reeling,
Tortured by intensest feeling —
   Like Prometheus, when the vultures
    Through his quivering vitals tore —

Swift I fled from death and darkness,
Through the streets of Baltimore!

No one near to save or love me!
No kind face to watch above me!
Though I heard the sound of footsteps,
Like the waves upon the shore,
Beating, beating, beating, beating!
Now advancing, now retreating —
With a dull and dreamy rhythm —
With a long, continuous roar —
Heard the sound of human footsteps,
In the streets of Baltimore!

There at length they found me lying,
Weak and 'wildered, sick and dying,
And my shattered wreck of being
To a kindly refuge bore!
But my woe was past enduring,
And my soul cast off its mooring,
Crying, as I floated outward,
"I am of the earth no more!
I have forfeited life's blessing
In the streets of Baltimore!"

Where wast thou, O Power Eternal!
When the fiery fiend, infernal,
   Beat me with his burning fasces,
      Till I sank to rise no more?
O, was all my life-long error
Crowded in that night of terror?
   Did my sin find expiation,
      Which to judgment went before,
Summoned to a dread tribunal,
      In the streets of Baltimore?

Nay, with deep, delirious pleasure,
I had drained my life's full measure,
   Till the fatal, fiery serpent,
      Fed upon my being's core!
Then with force and fire volcanic,
Summoning a strength Titanic,
   Did I burst the bonds that bound me —
      Battered down my being's door;
Fled, and left my shattered dwelling
      To the dust of Baltimore!

Gazing back without lamenting,
With no sorrowful repenting,

I can read my life's sad story
 In a light unknown before!
For there is no woe so dismal,
Not an evil so abysmal,
 But a rainbow arch of glory
  Spans the yawning chasm o'er!
 And across that Bridge of Beauty
  Did I pass from Baltimore!

In that grand, Eternal City,
Where the angel-hearts take pity
 On the sin which men forgive not,
  Or inactively deplore,
Earth has lost the power to harm me!
Death can never more alarm me,
 And I drink fresh inspiration
  From the Source which I adore —
Through my Spirit's apotheosis —
 That new birth in Baltimore!

Now no longer sadly yearning —
Love for love finds sweet returning —
 And there comes no ghostly raven,
  Tapping at my chamber door!

Calmly, in the golden glory,
I can sit and read life's story,
    For my soul from out that shadow
        Hath been lifted evermore —
    From that deep and dismal shadow,
        In the streets of Baltimore!

12

[As the following lecture is, in a certain sense, an introduction to Poe's " Farewell to Earth," it has been considered advisable to publish it in connection with the poem.]

THE MYSTERIES OF GODLINESS.

A LECTURE DELIVERED BY MISS LIZZIE DOTEN, AT CLINTON HALL, MONDAY, P. M., NOV. 2, 1863.

[Phonographically reported by Robert S. Moore.]

FOR several reasons, we must be as brief and comprehensive as possible in our remarks to-night. We do not intend to make any great intellectual effort, or to endeavor to astonish you with lofty strains of eloquence. We simply desire to present to you a few facts in connection with the poem about to be given, and we do this under the distinctive title of our discourse, — THE MYSTERIES OF GODLINESS.

As Godliness was a mystery in the past, so is it in the present. And why is it a mystery? Because men understand so little of the *practice* of Godliness.

Socrates was accustomed to say that "a man was always sufficiently eloquent in that which he clearly understood;" and thus a man will not look upon that as a mystery which is a part of his daily life, and with which he has become familiar through experience. But as it was in the days when Jesus lived and taught, or when Paul wrote his Epistle to Timothy, so Godliness, to the great mass of minds, remains a mystery. When Paul penned those words,—"Without controversy, great is the mystery of Godliness: God was manifest in the flesh, justified in the spirit, seen of angels, preached unto the Gentiles, believed on in the world, and received up into glory."—he referred particularly to the life and teachings of Jesus. We, however, give to the passage a more comprehensive and extended application. If the "Mystery of Godliness" was made manifest in the life of Jesus because of his divinity, then do we say to the men of the present day, "Beloved, now are ye also sons of God." And if "the Word was made flesh, and dwelt in the midst of men," in the person of Jesus of Nazareth, so that same Word is incarnated, in greater or less degree, in every human being, be he rich or poor, black or white, bond or free. In the same way, also, every one possessing a living soul is a manifestation of the mystery of Godliness. And when a man goes into his own nature, when he understands himself, when he reads the mysteries of his own being, when he looks away from his positive and earthly necessities up to his Divine possibilities, and sees how vast is the range, how infinite his capabilities, then he begins to understand something of the mysteries of Godliness. The Church has used this phraseology in the past, and knew not what it meant. She had "the form of Godliness," and yet in word and deed, ay, in very thought, she "denied the power thereof." Therefore it has been, in all past time, when there were some true and sincere souls in the Church, who made manifest, both by profession and practice, that in part at least, they comprehended the mystery of Godliness, which is the highest spirituality, — not Spiritualism, — and let it flow out into the beauty and harmony of perfect lives, the Church looked at them with a doubtful countenance. There was such a thing as being too holy, and the Church felt that such lives were a reproach to her self-righteousness and hypocrisy. She was not familiar with the manifestation of true Godliness, and consequently looked upon it as something that threatened her internal peace, and the success of her stereotyped plan of salvation. Therefore it was, that the voice of condemnation was raised against Michael De Molinos, Fenelon, Madame Guyon, and the whole host of Quietists and Reformers. By dim forecastings of the soul, and heroic struggling with flesh and sense, they had learned something of that holy mystery. It was that which could not be translated into human language. It could not be written in books, but it was that which was to be felt in the soul, and made manifest in the life. Godliness, true spirituality, cannot find expression in words, and so it must of necessity manifest its Divine beauty in the life.

But what is the idea we intend to convey when we use the term "Godliness"? Who is God, from whose name this word is simply a derivative? Godliness is the manifestation of his spirit and power in the soul of man, yet it is not God. Who, then, is He! We must look into the lexicon of every human heart to find our reply; for each one worships his own Ideal of Deity according to the revelation of Truth which he receives, and to the capacity of his spirit to comprehend. The old philosophers sought for God in all the external world; they also went down into the mysteries of the spirit, as far as philosophy could sound its mighty depths, and yet they could not fathom his infinite nature. Although form and an external are necessary to man as a completion of his idea, yet when he reasons deeply concerning Deity, he cannot arrive at any satisfactory conclusions concerning his personality; he can only worship him as a principle, as a presence, and a power. Man, in his insignificance, can only look up to that superior Intelligence, which manifests itself throughout Nature, and worship either in the silence of the heart or in the inadequate articulations of human speech. The finite never did as yet compass and comprehend the Infinite. And before that majestic question which all the Ages have sought in vain to answer, before that mighty Oracle whose essence and nature have never been understood, man might as well remain dumb.

But where, you ask, shall man find his highest manifestation of Deity? How shall he know and understand God, so that he may attain unto the true mystery of Godliness? The most of God that you can know is through your own souls. Your neighbor may speak unto you of the influences which flow in upon him from the great Soul of all: you can only listen, but cannot comprehend, unless there is something of the same spirit — of the same Divine life within you. But as you grow in goodness and spirituality, you comprehend more clearly the truth which Jesus, the greatest Medium the world ever knew, spoke to the ears of men, when he said, "God is a Spirit, and they that worship him must worship him in spirit and in truth." Therefore our definition of Godliness is spirituality, the influence of God felt in the soul and made manifest in the life of man. Just in proportion as this principle or power is realized in the hearts of men, they approach nearer unto Deity; they see more of his perfect life: they understand more of his ways; they leave speculations concerning his personality, and go away to those great generalizations whereby a man's soul grows comprehensive and universal in its sympathies, and beholds the operations of the Infinite mind in all things. Thus, as Jesus was a manifestation of that Godliness or spirituality, the self-same Divine power—the "Divine in the human" is manifest in every sentient being.

And here we approach a mighty truth, in whose majestic presence we feel inclined to lay aside our dusty sandals; for the place whereon we stand seems holy ground. While studying the mysteries of our own being, we find that necessarily we worship Everlasting Truth, in whatever form it may be presented. We go away from limitations, we go away from sects and creeds, from tottering institutions and the musty theologies of the past, and stand face to face with that fresher revelation of Deity in the heart. Then it is that man feels there are primary and fundamental truths lying at the basis of all philosophy and all religion, and only as he builds upon these broad foundations can he rear a glorious superstructure against which all the winds of changing theories, and the descending floods of mere speculative philosophy, will not be able to prevail. As man, like one initiated into the mysteries of Masonry, enters into this lodge of freedom, he begins to believe in himself. No man can have faith in God who has no faith in himself; that is the first step towards the Divine. You take that step in the secret of the soul when you first acknowledge the "Divine in the human," and confess its supporting influence.

For instance, two men may be standing on the borders of a precipice: below, there is the deep ravine; opposite, the other side of the mountain. They look far down and see rough, ragged points of rocks, and far, far below, the floods boiling white with foam. Over this abyss there is but one slight, frail bridge, and that is the trunk of a single tree. One man says, "Since we must pass over, I will precede. I know that I can go; I *will* go." That man has faith in himself. He plants his feet firmly; he looks upward, and passes safely over. The second says, "I do not believe that I can go; I fear I shall fall." He totters on, trembling, until he reaches the middle, and then cries out, "O Lord, Lord, help me!" So surely as he utters that cry, faithless in his own power, that man must fall.

And thus it is with human souls. They are standing here, in earthly life, gazing across the great abyss of the Future. It is dark and terrible below. They cannot clearly understand what fate awaits them, but they see the strait and narrow way before them. If a man plants his feet firmly, and says, "I can, and I will," it is the greatest possible acknowledgement of his faith in God. That man has stepped upon the threshold of the mysteries of Godliness; those mysteries will be made clearer and more apparent to his soul as he advances. But if, with craven soul, he says, "I know not what to do. I will wait for God's providences, and let them come as they may; for of myself I can do nothing," — if he trust to the vicarious atonement and an external Deity, and does nothing for his own salvation, — if, in making oral prayers to the Lord of the Universe, he forgets to "worship God in spirit," and loses the vitalizing consciousness of the Divine within his own being, that man will assuredly err; he will continually go astray, for externally he has "the form of Godliness," but practically and internally he denies "the power thereof."

The world to-day is standing, in a certain sense, in that same position. Men are lifting up their hands, and crying, "Lord, Lord!" believing that they shall thus enter into the kingdom, while within their own beings there is a broad region of spiritual mysteries unknown and unexplored. Here

and there are instances where souls, driven by the
action of their own importunate reason, — ay, we
may say, by simple common sense, — have turned
aside from creeds and theories, and have inquired
earnestly of Nature and of the God within. It is
refreshing at times to find such a soul : one that
believes in the inspiration of the living Word, incarnated in all flesh, and made apparent throughout
the universe, — not a Pantheist, believing in the
manifestation of Deity in Nature alone, and in
nothing higher, but realizing that the creation is
the perceptible and external revelation of Deity ;
believing, with the German philosopher Fichte, that
" there is a Divine Idea pervading this visible universe ; which visible universe is indeed but its
symbol and sensible manifestation, having in itself
no meaning, or even true existence, independent
of it. To the mass of men this Divine Idea lies
hidden ; yet, to discern it, to seize it, and live
wholly in it, is the condition of all genuine virtue,
knowledge, freedom, and the end, therefore, of all
spiritual effort in every age." He who lives and
dwells in this Idea, enters into the mysteries of
Godliness. All divine things are exceedingly sim-

ple when they are known. It is because men are
looking too high that they do not receive the
living inspirations of the Truth; they turn away
from themselves, and neglect to observe the manifestation of the spirit within their own being.
They look upon their brother man or sister woman,
and forget to exercise that broad charity which sees
the spirit struggling with the flesh, or feebly breast-
ing the wild waves of a tempestuous life, simply
because it was thus constituted and surrounded.
Men commonly judge from their own individual
stand-point, instead of going away back to the Divinity of the inner life, and from its pure eyes
looking into the heart of their erring brother or
sister. He who simply criticizes the man, and
judges him by the limitations of his own life, errs
greatly. But he who looks beyond and behind
him, sees that there are truths, and principles, and
powers, and loving, earnest spirits, who are endeavoring to make manifest their inspiration through
him; and although he may be changeable in his
nature, although he may be erratic and wandering,
it is only through the excess of power that cannot
find an appropriate manifestation through such an
organization.

And such a one was he of whom we speak to-night, — that erratic genius, Edgar A. Poe. The mysteries of Godliness, — not of morality, as the world understands it, — confounded him. He could see more clearly than most of men. He looked out into the vast arcana of Nature, and his soul trembled before the majestic revelation. He knew not how to express, in any adequate form of speech, those great and mighty thoughts which rose and shone, like stars of wondrous beauty, in his soul; he knew not how to give his burning inspirations a manifestation through his life and being.

Edgar A. Poe was a medium. "A medium!" you say. "He himself would scorn the name; and we, who knew him, deny it." But of what was he a medium? We do not confine ourselves to that definition of the term given by modern Spiritualists. He was a medium for the general inspiration which sets like a current of living fire through the universe. No special, no individual spirit wrought directly upon him, but he felt the might and majesty of occult forces from the world of causes, and trembled beneath their influence. He was a medium, not to disembodied spirits, only so far as

13

mind acts upon mind by the great law of unity, and in the same way was he psychologically affected by spirits in the body. He had a peculiarly sensitive and impressible nature, and in the mysteries of a spirituality which he did not seek to comprehend, he was easily wrought upon by the minds around him. Not but what he possessed self-will; not, indeed, that he lacked that firmness, whereby, when his soul was aroused, he could repel such influences. But his nature was so finely strung that every harsh word, every unkindly discord, grated and thrilled through his entire being, so that oftentimes it would seem as though he would beat down the wall of clay to give his spirit freedom, and to escape forever from the inharmonious influences of the world, — from the presence of those by whom he was so little understood.

It is difficult to comprehend such natures, for they are not common. But, alas for such! They have no choice but to be denizens of this world, and all the rough, sharp angles of rude Humanity seem continually to wound and irritate their sensitiveness, torturing them almost to madness. And yet there is a deep, strong under-current to their lives.

There is a beautiful spirituality which leads men
to perceive that there is a power in the universe
which balances all these inequalities and apparent
inharmonies of human beings; and so, although
they are set at variance with the world in certain
portions of their nature, yet they are rewarded in
others. Edgar A. Poe possessed the power of
retiring from external things into the mysteries of
the spirit. The greatest authors and musical composers the world ever knew, were those whose
favorite pursuit so completely absorbed them that
all external things were excluded, and they forgot,
while their inspirations were upon them, what
manner of men they were, — forgot the necessities
of the flesh, and all the surroundings of their daily
lives. Such men could understand our meaning,
when we say that Edgar A. Poe lived much in
his inner life, and there, as in the experience
of the soul-rapt and inspired Boehmen, glorious
revelations of the sublime and the beautiful were
made manifest unto him. The common forms of
human speech were inadequate for expression;
therefore he seized upon the secret harmony of
words, and strung them like flashing gems on the

golden line of his thought, weaving them into wild,
strange metaphors, oftentimes so bewildering and
dazzling, that the common mind could only feel
the charm without comprehending the mystery.
Like Ezekiel in his vision, he beheld the wondrous
"living creatures, and the wheels," and as they
were represented, so did he describe them; but
the mind of the reader must be in a similar state
of illumination in order to clearly understand his
meaning. There were seasons when he seemed to
enter into a peaceful alliance with earth and all
harmonious and beautiful things. Yet when his
peculiarly sensitive nature was startled and aroused,
he turned back to this Valhalla of his soul, and
there he found another element of peace, — a
strange, paradoxical peace, which comes through
the herculean efforts of the soul to clamber up the
rugged heights of destiny, — such peace as is
given unto souls, when the angel, with a flaming
sword, drives them from the Eden places of this
world back into the mysteries of their being, in
order that from their bloody sweat and bitter
agony they may wring out great songs of moving
inspiration, and reveal to mankind generally the

wondrous world of ideas and causes which lies beyond the limits of sense and the range of external observation.

All such are men of Destiny. They are compelled over the ways which they tread. The world looks upon them, and cannot understand them; men consider them as anomalies and strange inconsistencies; as abnormal manifestations of the spirit. Yet "for this cause came they into the world;" and as poets, and artists, and musical composers are born with the undeveloped elements of their genius within them, so particular souls, in close connection with the spiritual world, who are continually receiving direct impressions and revelations from the sphere of causes, are born such from their cradle; and thus the mystery of spirituality or godliness, as the world passes on generation after generation, is becoming more and more apparent in the lives and experiences of men. When we speak of spirituality, do not consider that we mean modern Spiritualism, as understood by the world, which has furnished any amount of sheep's clothing to the wolves who desire to prey upon the lambs in the unguarded fold of Humanity. Neither do we mean

13 *

that inflated spirituality, which, in its zeal for re-
form, and contempt for ceremonies and limitations,
rushes to extremes, and, deceiving itself, "uses its
liberty as an occasion to the flesh." But we do
mean that living principle, which makes itself manifest in high-toned souls, whose sublime aspirations
exalt the whole life above the common level of
Humanity. It may come out as a fitful and glim-
mering light, but it shows that the Divine inspiration is there, and all men, when they perceive it,
are ready to acknowledge it as genuine. Whatever
is truly good, glorious, or divine, that which pos-
sesses in itself real merit and inspiration, cannot
fail to find a responsive echo. And thus was it
with the writings of Poe. When, from the glowing
fire-crypts of his soul, he wrought out, with master
strokes, his " Raven," and gave it to the world,
men felt that there was the ring of true genius.
And, although it was the utterance of a nature at
variance with its earthy surroundings, and tortured
by its own sensibility, yet because of its gloomy
grandeur and euphonious rhythm, the poem could
not fail to be appreciated.

Such natures cannot live long in the flesh. They

are like two-edged swords, which wear upon the
scabbard. There is ever an unseen hand upon the
hilt, and finally, when the word of command is
given, the sword is drawn, and becomes a most
effective instrument in the hand of Everlasting
Truth; then the individual nature that has so long
battled the stormy elements of mortal life first per-
ceives its advantages, and in the triumphant exulta-
tion which spirits always feel when freed from the
fetters of mortality, it exclaims, "O Death! where
is thy sting? O Grave! where is thy victory?"
That diviner spirituality which was obscured by
the flesh, which was crushed down by earthly circumstances, at length frees itself, and starts up
in all its majesty and glory. But the mysterious
growth and development of the spirit does not
end here.

Perhaps in this connection we may present to
you certain points from which you will feel obliged
to dissent. They may seem like vague theories
and wild speculations, yet they are truths which
you are yet to realize in your eternal experience,
—truths which this one of whom we speak will
present to you in repetition to-night.

There is a power in man which is closely connected with the things of external life, and draws
inspiration from nature and the associations of
his fellow-men. There is a power, also, in every
human being superior to the spirit, and that is
the soul, or innermost life — which is a divine
and indestructible principle. When, therefore, the
garment of flesh is laid aside, — when the mortal
puts on its immortality, — the spirit goes forth pre-
cisely as it is. If it has been under the influence
of ungoverned passion; if it has striven, through
mad ambition, to attain to some cherished ideal, still
does it feel that impetus, and its earthly longings
and aspirations must pass away through a gradual
transformation. You may dissent from this, but
the change of the earthly garment does not effect
a radical change in the spirit. And thus, as the
spirit of Edgar A. Poe started forth on its celestial
journey, all that bound him to earth still held a
certain degree of influence over him. "Life is
one eternal progress," and only by progression
and the gradual development of his nobler nature
could he outlive that bondage. In many respects
he had loved life and the things of earth. In

his intercourse with men he could not free himself from "the sins which did so easily beset him." Neither could he restrain that sensitiveness and irritability of nature which so often destroyed the peace of his outer and inner life, and therefore he must necessarily outgrow that in higher conditions, and under more favorable influences. As he gradually attained to a sublimer consciousness of the beautiful and true, much of the wild and fitful fire peculiar to his genius departed from him, and there came in its stead a majestic flow of inspiration, solemn and grand as the music of the spheres. He saw that there were harmonious relations awaiting him; and as his soul was rich in sympathy and love, he aspired to those conditions, and he could not rest until he had attained unto them. The hinderance to his perfect peace was in his own spirit, and he realized it. It was for him the commencement of a mighty struggle, —

"When the golden bowl, — life's token, —
Into shining shards was broken."

It would seem, then, as though conscious of his strength, he stood up like a spiritual giant, exclaiming, "I am free! At last I am free!" There was a complete expansion of his being as he drank in the celestial air. He could not clearly understand the mysteries by which he was surrounded, but he knew that there was a latent energy in his soul, which, being more fully developed, would wrestle with these mighty problems until he made the solution his own. As year after year, marking great and important changes in human experience, rolled on, men who remembered Poe as he was, said, "Now he rests from life's labor; now he sins and sorrows no more."

But they did not know upon what a mighty battle-field he stood, neither could they understand through what fires of purification he was passing. But there he stood, contending bravely, not once losing faith in his soul's possibilities, and pressing earnestly forward to the desired consummation. And in this he was not alone. O, no! There was with him a whole host of moral heroes, who, conscious of their power to win the victory, and quickened by the inspirations which they received from that higher state of being, were striving, by the excelsior movement of the soul, to attain to those glory-encircled heights from whence they could look calmly down upon the plane of their earthly existence.

Thus it was that, as they gradually arose higher and higher in the scale of being, he and they could perceive that all sin, and sorrow, and evil ended at length in blessing, and that truths, which were dim and indistinct, which seemed aught but truths, came out into clear and shining light, and in their heavens were stars of the first magnitude. Thus, also, as he toiled on he became versed in the mysteries of the spirit, not in mere moralities — for true religion, godliness or spirituality, is the full, free, and complete development of man's entire being, both in the intellectual and moral. Science and literature, art and religion, have been separated by mankind, because they did not understand the true mystery of Godliness.

But in that higher life one of the first lessons taught to the soul is, that all things have their uses. Even the low, animal passions, leading man into error, into sin, sensuality, and evil, will thereby teach him lessons of wisdom ; will teach him to avoid the false and the untrue, and also that there were rocks and quicksands upon which his bark had almost foundered, and which in the future he must avoid. Whether it be these lower passions, or the intellectual and moral, still each must have its own appropriate manifestation.

And as all these capacities for growth and perception belong not to the body but to the spirit, so the spirit, sweeping away into the great Eternity, bears up all these powers of its wondrous mechanism with it, and the vision. of Ezekiel is realized; for " the living creature being lifted up, the wheels are lifted up also."

Each organ of the brain has its own magnetic circle, touching the one upon another like the mechanism of a watch, and all governed by the mainspring, which is the internal consciousness of man, the central power of his being. This order in the change from the mortal to the immortal is not lost, but finds a more harmonious surrounding. Thus, when the spirit has ascended, with its increased power, with its superior opportunities for observation and investigation of all the truths of the universe, it learns this most important truth, — that not in *one* direction, but in *all*, the spirit shall find its most free and perfect development.

Thus having become familiar with the conditions of the higher life, the one of whom we speak realized that it was not in the poetic element of his being alone that he was to find inspiration, not in smooth flowing numbers or cunning arrangements of human speech, but in the grand harmony of the living whole — the perfect accord of his entire being. It was necessary, in passing forth from the flesh, that he should learn this simple lesson. He has endeavored by all the powers of his nature to make its application; and he has succeeded. This night he gives his "Farewell to Earth." Not that he is to be divided forever in his interest from Humanity, but, no longer incited by restlessness or ambition, to express in rhythmic numbers the fiery thought within, no longer drawn by the sordid interests of this earthly life, he can gaze down upon this lower world and influence the minds of men, and still be above them. He can still minister, as an Everlasting Truth and living power, to the needs of Humanity; but as Poe, the individual, he is willing to be forgotten. His personality, as far as human recognition is concerned, can end here. He cares not that "this poor, paltry *me* should be spun

14

out into Infinity." He says: "Let my soul speak, which is the Divine Power. I have realized in myself the mysteries of Godliness, and know now that I too am Divine. I have merged and lost my will in the Great Will of the universe. I know now what heaven is; it is beauty, perfection, harmony. I would live forever in that celestial air, and draw in the vitalizing influences of truth. I do not desire to go down to the lowly homes of earth, nor to mingle with men in their contentions and selfish interests. I know that there is a Power guarding and guiding all things, and I can trust those whom I have loved, or those for whom I have cared, in that Almighty Hand. Whatever mysterious manifestation of wisdom on the part of Divine Providence comes to Humanity, I can say now, 'It is well! Let the will of that Power be done!' I have then no work to perform for you. I have only to carry with me through the vast Eternity an open nature, that I may receive truths, and, in passing onward, transmit them to those who are to follow after me."

Thus it is with all great and earnest souls. "The mystery of Godliness," or true spirituality, as an impelling and inspiring power, is behind them, making itself manifest through their being. It also stands before them, beckoning them on the way. It may be they have natures of steel and fire, and that a thought electric strikes upon the heart, and sits, a mania, on the brain. But still they feel that power impelling and persuading, and finally when they perceive that the grand current of human events is tending towards the great ocean of Infinite Truth, they are willing to let their own peculiarities and characteristic tendencies also flow on in the great stream, and so harmony is at length established, not only with themselves but all.

The lesson of Poe's life, in itself, was worth much to Humanity. In coming time, others besides ourselves will dissect and analyze his peculiar nature, and present it, even as we have, to men, as an instance of that Spirit which was "made manifest in the flesh, which was seen of angels, was preached by inspired lips to Humanity, believed on in the world, and received up into glory." Great, indeed, is the mystery of Godliness! great in the light of the human lives that come and go upon the broad arena of earthly existence. Great, also, is that mystery made manifest in those spirits who go forth from the flesh, and feeling the Divine inspiration stirring within them, seek for life, — Eternal Life, — in order that they may grow and expand to the fulness of their spiritual being, having within themselves a quenchless thirst for the harmonious and the beautiful. They are true to the great law of spirit, for whether in Time or Eternity, it may still be said that, —

" Within the heart of man there is a constant yearning
    For something higher, holier, unattained, —
Upward and onward, from the present turning,
    Yet resting never when a point is gained.
Some unseen spirit evermore the soul is urging
    Through childish weakness and ambitious youth ;
And day by day all souls are still converging
    Nearer and nearer to the Central Source of Truth.
Youth cuts a foothold in the Rock of Ages ;
    The hope of Fame and Glory lures him on his way,
And, pondering o'er the works of ancient sages,
    He catches glimpses of a brighter day.
Alas ! but toilsome is the way, and dreary,
    To him who has no high and holy aim,
And, pausing on Life's threshold, sad and weary,
    He casts away the laurel wreath of Fame." *

Thus was it with Poe. Not clearly discerning

* These lines, with those at the close of the lecture, are quoted from one of my written poems.

the purposes of life, he did not bend his efforts to one high and holy aim. His nature was wandering and erratic. This is also *his* present view of his earthly life. "He has cast away his laurel wreath of fame," and now upon his brow, burning brightly with the glories of the celestial sphere, is an olive wreath of peace. He stands now as a majestic soul, self-poised and harmonious. Yet he has not lost aught of the brilliancy and fire of his genius.

Edgar A. Poe was mighty in the flesh; and in the spirit he is mightier far. His manifestations will yet come to mankind, but not as from the individual. They will speak to your souls; they will breathe in words of fire from the lips of Humanity, as inspirations from the Higher Life, rather than as the utterances of him who was once known among men as EDGAR A. POE.

"O, ever thus have Earth's most noble-hearted
    Gone calmly upward to their place above !
And when their footsteps from the earth departed,
    Have left their works of genius or of love.
For Aspiration is the moral lever, raising
    The earnest spirit to its destined height ;
But Inspiration only comes from gazing
    Upon the perfect Source of Life and Light!"

14 *

FAREWELL TO EARTH.

[The following poem purports to be Poe's final farewell to Earth.
It was given in the city of New York, Monday evening, Nov. 2, 1863.]

I.

FAREWELL! Farewell!
Like the music of a bell
Floating downward to the dell —
  Downward from some Alpine height,
  While the sunset-embers bright,
  Fade upon the hearth of night;
So my spirit, voiceless — breathless, —
Indestructible and deathless,
From the heights of Life Elysian gives to Earth
    my parting song;
  Downward through the star-lit spaces,
  Unto Earth's most lowly places,
Like the sun-born strains of Memnon, let the music
    float along,

With a wild and wayward rhythm, with a movement deep and strong.
"Come up higher!" cry the angels. — This must
be my parting song.

Earth! O Earth! thou art my Mother.
Mortal man! thou art my Brother.
We have shared a mutual sorrow, we have known
a common birth;
Yet with all my soul's endeavor,
I will sunder, and forever,
Every tie of human passion that can bind my soul
to Earth —
Every slavish tie that binds me to the things of
little worth.
"Come up higher!" cry the angels: "come! and
bid farewell to Earth."

I would bear a love Platonic to the souls in
earthly life;
I would give a sign Masonic to the heroes in the
strife;
I have been their fellow-craftsman, bound appren-
tice to that Art.
Whereby Life, that cunning draughtsman, builds
his temple in the heart.

But with Earth no longer mated, I have passed
    the First Degree;
I have been initiated to the second mystery.
O, its high and holy meaning not one soul shall
    fail to see!
Now, with loftiest aspirations, onward through the
    worlds I march,
Through the countless constellations, upward to the
    Royal Arch.
"Come up higher!" cry the angels: "come up to
    the Royal Arch."

II.

Farewell! Farewell!
Like the tolling of a bell,
Sounding forth some funeral knell, —
   Tolling with a sad refrain,
   Not for those who rest from pain,
   But for those who still remain;
So sweet pathos would I borrow
From the loving lips of Sorrow,
Weaving in a plaintive minor with the cadence
    of my song,
For the souls that lonely languish,

For the hearts that break with anguish,

For the weak ones and the tempted, who must
  sin and suffer long;

For the hosts of living martyrs, groaning 'neath
  some ancient wrong;

For the cowards and the cravens, who in guilt
  alone are strong.

But from all Earth's woe and sadness,

All its folly and its madness,

I would never strive to save you, or avert the
  evil blow;

Even if I would, I could not,

Even if I could, I would not

Turn the course of Time's great river, in its grand,
  majestic flow;

Grapple with those mighty causes whose results I
  may not know:

All Life's sorrows end in blessing, as the future yet
  shall show.

From Life's overflowing beaker I have drained the
  bitter draught,

Changing to a maddening ichor in my being as I
  quaffed.

I have felt the hot blood rushing o'er its red and
  rameous path,
Like the molten lava, gushing in its wild, volcanic
  wrath ;
Like a bubbling, boiling Geyser, in the regions of
  the pole ;
Like a Scylla or Charybdis, threatening to ingulf
  my soul.
O, for all such fire-wrought natures let my rhythmic
  numbers toll !
Vulnerable, like Achilles, only in one fatal part,
I was wounded, by Life's arrows, in the head, but
  not the heart.
" Come up higher!" cried the angels ; — and I hastened to depart.

III.

Farewell ! farewell !
Like a merry marriage-bell,
Pealing with a tuneful swell,
  Telling, in a joyful strain,
  With a whispered, sweet refrain,
  Of the hearts no longer twain ;
So no longer cursed and fated,
Fondly loved and truly mated,

I can pour my inspirations, free as Orpheus,
    through my strain.
    Gifted with a sense of seeing
    Far beyond my earthly being,
I can feel I have not suffered, loved, and hoped,
    and feared in vain ;
Every earthly sin and sorrow I can only count as
    gain :
I can chant a grand " Te Deum " o'er the record
    of my pain.

    Ye who grope in darkness blindly,
    Ye who seek a refuge kindly,
Ye upon whose hearts the ravens — ghostly ravens
    — perch and prey,
    Listen ! for the bells are ringing,
    Tuneful as the angels singing,
Ringing in the glorious morning of your spirit's
    marriage-day,
When the soul, no longer fettered to the feeble
    form of clay,
To a high, harmonious union, soars, elate with hope
    away.

Where the iris arch of Beauty bridges o'er celestial
skies,
Where the golden line of Duty, like a living path-
way lies,
Where the gonfalons of Glory float upon the fra-
grant air,
Ye who read Life's lengthening story, find a Royal
Chapter there.
Ye shall see how men and nations o'er the ways
of life advance;
Ye shall watch the constellations in their mazy,
mystic dance;
And the Central Sun shall greet you — greet you
with a golden glance.
O, for souls in Life Eternal let the bells in glad-
ness ring!
Bind the wreath of orange blossoms, and the
wedding garment bring.
"Come up higher!" cry the angels. — Let the bells
in gladness ring.

IV.

Farewell! Farewell!
Like the chiming of the bells,
Which a tale of triumph tells:

As the news in tuneful notes,
Leaping from the brazen throats,
On the startled ether floats; —
So in freedom, great and glorious,
Over flesh and sense victorious,
Does the Spirit leap the barrier which across its
    pathway lies!
Greater far than royal Cæsar,
Fearless as the northern Æsir,
Drawn by Love's celestial magnet, winged with
    faith and hope it flies,
Upward o'er the starry pathway, leading onward
    through the skies,
To the land of Light and Beauty, where no bud
    of promise dies.

There, through all the vast Empyrean,
Wafted, as on gales Hesperian,
Comes the stirring cry of "Progress"! telling of
    the yet to be.
Tuneful as a seraph's lyre,
"Come up higher! Come up higher!"
Cry the hosts of holy angels; "learn the heavenly
    Masonry:

15

Life is one eternal progress: enter, then, the Third
      Degree ; —
Ye who long for light and wisdom seek the Inner
      Mystery!

Thus, O Sons of Earth, I leave you! — leave you
      for that higher light ;
And my charge is now, Receive you all my part-
      ing words aright:
Human passion, mad ambition, bound me to this
      lower Earth,
Even in my changed condition — even in my higher
      birth.
But, by earnest, firm endeavor, I have gained a
      height sublime ;
And I ne'er again — no, never! — shall be *bound*
      to Space or Time ;
I have conquered! and forever! Let the bells in
      triumph chime!
" Come up higher! " cry the angels: " come up to
      the Royal Arch!
Come and join the Past Grand Masters, in the
      Soul's progressive march,
O, thou neophyte of Wisdom! Come up to the
      Royal Arch! "

Sons of Earth! where'er ye dwell,
Break Temptation's magic spell!
Truth is Heaven, and Falsehood, Hell!
Lawless Lust a demon fell!
Sons of Earth! where'er ye dwell, —
In this Heaven, or in this Hell, —
When ye hear the solemn swell
Of Creation's mighty bell
Sounding forth Time's funeral knell,
Ye shall meet me where I dwell; —
Until then — FAREWELL! FAREWELL!

www.ingramcontent.com/pod-product-compliance
Lightning Source LLC
Chambersburg PA
CBHW030547040726
47497CB00008B/2609